The Wall Of Shame

Ulrika Lorenz

Dedication

To all children, exploited to human trafficking for sexual and commercial exploitation.

What doesn't kill you...

We all know the famous quote

"What doesn't kill you makes you stronger."

But that's not entirely true...

What doesn't kill you lets you live to fight another day and learn from your mistakes.

So if anything - it makes you more cautious, broadens your perspective, and guides you to what matters the most.

So;

"What doesn't kill you makes you wiser."

And in my opinion, wisdom beats strength any day.

Denise Lorenz

Legal Notices

No part of this publication may be reproduced or transmitted in any material form (including photocopying or storing in any medium by electronic means) without the written permission of the author Ulrika Lorenz.

The purpose of this book is to educate, entertain and provide information on the subject matter covered. All attempts have been made to verify the information at the time of publication. The author does not assume any responsibility for errors, omissions or other interpretations of the subject matter. The purchaser or reader of this book assumes responsibility for the use of this material and information. The author assumes no responsibility or liability on behalf of any purchaser or reader of this book.

Copyright © 2021 Ulrika Lorenz

All rights reserved.

ISBN: 9798532187030

Foreword

It was at my sister's Hawaiian themed birthday party that I first met Ulrika. What struck me was how interesting she and her entrepreneurial endeavours were.

After meeting again on several other occasions, I saw that her skills went beyond just being an entrepreneur. I came to see that she was prepared to put her investments into one extremely philanthropic venture – to stop human trafficking.

During one of our conversations, she said, 'We have to take human rights to another level and start to talk about human responsibilities." This struck a chord with me because we cannot talk about rights without talking about responsibilities. Being responsible is about serving our community and supporting those who have no voice.

When Ulrika asked me to read her new book, Wall Of Shame, I knew I would learn more about her and her passion and purpose. I learned that working for human rights is to believe in the impossible, to sometimes lose hope and continue regardless, seeking a glimmer of light in fragile progress. The book inspires curiosity and a desire for adventure where nothing is impossible, just as one would expect an entrepreneur driven by her goals.

Sweden is doing a lot of work to tackle human trafficking, so it delights me to read a book from this intrepid entrepreneur that demonstrates and puts into action smart solutions to support projects that mean that others can live with some respect and dignity.

Taking the whole family on year-long volunteer projects may not be for everyone, but Ulrika shows that it is entirely possible. I admire her desire to influence the next generation so positively. She makes you realise that all of us are part of the demand for human trafficking. Her writing calls to you as a reader to immediately roll up your sleeves, find your purpose and be a change for good.

In my work, I have seen what pornography, prostitution, and other forms of human trafficking do to society, people and relationships. It is an ugly truth, and we need more brave people working against it. This book shows you where you, too, can start to make a difference.

In reading Wall Of Shame, I can see that I am not alone. I am reminded that there are many great champions in the world fighting for human rights and that I am part of a community with a common vision. It would be wonderful to see more entrepreneurs incorporating social pathos into their businesses. I hope that the book inspires them to consider more about how we can all create "An empathic world without human trafficking".

Wall of Shame should be read by anyone who seeks inspiration and motivation to start working against modern slavery but do not know where to start.

Per-Anders Sunesson, Former Ambassador at Large to Combat Human Trafficking

Table of contents

Chapter 1	1
Chapter 2	17
Chapter 3	33
Chapter 4	47
Chapter 5	65
Chapter 6	79
Chapter 7	91
Chapter 8	105
Chapter 9	123
Chapter 10	143
Chapter 11	159
Chapter 12	171
Chapter 13	181
Chapter 14	193
Chapter 15	205
Chapter 16	219
Celebration and next steps	225
Author's profile	231
Acknowledgements, Thank you and Namaste	235
References	239

What others are saying about the wall of shame

"I want to read more! Your writing is so open and honest! I can´t tell you how many times I stopped and reread a sentence or a phrase, and it really made me think about my own life! So inspiring, Ulrika! Keep writing!!!

Deborah

"I LOVE your book. It is so inspiring !!!"

Louise

"It feels like if I have been on a long, long journey and come back with lots of important experiences and new inspiring thoughts. I am deeply touched."

Gunnel

"I just want to say that I think you are so incredibly brave and strong who dare to be so honest, open and to expose your most inner thoughts in your book. All respect 💕 "

Denise

Wall of Shame
Introduction

Every author, I suppose, writes to open the eyes of their readers to other worlds - places of possibility and opportunity. It is in the furthest reaches of the imagination that we can visualise greater things, deliver new knowledge and insights and, dare I say it, change the world.

Imagine being able to change, influence and inspire through the written word. This has been my dream for a long time. I started my book journey with the intention of writing a novel about human trafficking for sexual purposes, based on the many human stories and experiences I encountered during my travels.

Instead, I dived into my stories so that I could show you what brought me to this point. And how I came to see strange contrasts between their world of slavery, the shame attached, and how ashamed I felt about my contribution to the problem. In some way, we are all prisoners. Some can remove the bars if only they knew how, while others are forever trapped in a living hell. This is what shame does.

When I started to write, I realised how powerful this could be. If you are not a famous artist, actor or journalist, or have not already written a recognisably successful book, it is perhaps a little presumptuous to think that your book may become a bestseller, or even that it will ever get published.

If you let the fear of what others may think stand in your way, you will miss a world-changing opportunity to make the world a slightly better place. So, the question is, how do you start?

Well, you think about what you have actually achieved in recent years, and write down your scattered anecdotes in various notebooks and on bits of scrap paper. My book didn't happen overnight. I started this book project a couple of years ago with the intention of capturing a chronological account of what has happened since I started the organisation, *Do Good Now*. It was, as I said, going to be a novel. But instead, it has become something that is real, impactful and, I believe, something that will get people like you thinking of how you can be a part of the solution.

There were many times during this process that I thought about why I wanted to work for human rights at all, and against modern slavery, especially human trafficking for commercial and sexual purposes. It is as if this endeavour found, in me, the perfect person with the drive, energy and passion for doing the work.

Writing this book became an inner journey, taking me back in time, and thrusting me forward with my vision for the future. This deep dive into my own emotional history revealed something I recognised in the women I had met, albeit in different situations and continents. Common to us all was, surprisingly, shame. Whether the shame is rooted in humiliation and exploitation, or poor self-esteem, it exudes the scent of *'not being good enough'* for the world.

My stories show you glimpses into the lives of people who surrounded me during my upbringing, fragments through my years of education, and lessons from life's winding paths. Along the way, I began to examine my core values, truths, and views on life, and that never-ending question, why we are here on earth?

Furthermore, my intention with these chapters is to raise the following question, "Why are we still too uncivilised to achieve the goal of sustainability and social responsibility where human rights are fully respected?" It is time for us to take the awareness and practise of human rights to a new level and start discussing our shared human responsibility. According to the United Nations, every human being is born free. So, let's start making this a truth. Now.

Finally, the book is a call for a collective awakening and common consciousness. We live as if there were not enough, with a constant need for more of everything, whether it is beauty, consumption, convenience or success. The economy behind the scarcity of resources still governs large parts of our existence. When we realise that we are all part of the demand that breeds human trafficking, we have come one step closer to a kinder world.

With the time and capital invested in preventive work, information dissemination, and direct hands-on projects for more human freedom, I hope the non-profit organisation *Do Good Now* will be my life's best investment. Moreover, the return is non-monetary, as human lives are not measured in hard currency, but hold a far greater value.

All profits go to projects

The entire profits from the sale of this book fund anti-trafficking work, poverty alleviation programmes, and relief projects for refugees or people who are otherwise disadvantaged by human rights violations.

Chapter 1

"The first lesson of economics is scarcity: there is never enough of anything to fully satisfy all those who want it. The first lesson of politics is to disregard the first lesson of economics." Thomas Sowell

Scarcity and Demand

As I stood in line, waiting to board the aircraft, the couple caught my attention. Two people deeply in love, who just had eyes for each other. They couldn't help but look at and touch each other.

She watched him with admiration while he put his hand in hers and gave her another soft kiss. The world might fall apart, or the flight could be further delayed. They could lose their jobs and all their belongings. They couldn't care less about what was happening around them, as long as they had each other.

Their brains were completely hijacked by hormones, which made them feel that they had everything they needed — each other.

What does this love story have to do with the economics of scarcity of resources and the demand for products and services? My point is that we only demand something we need or want, whether that desire is created by ourselves or by external marketing forces. If we add habits and addiction to the picture, it is a no-brainer to see that our desire for our favourite Caffè Latte awakens our demand for more coffee shops, and causes us to experience a scarcity of good coffee when travelling to a place where there is no fancy coffee shop.

The couple at the airport did not experience any scarcity of love. Their experience was that they had enough of everything. They would eat whatever was available, just to satiate their hunger, should it occur, but they probably would not have time to make complicated meals with exotic ingredients. It would take time from their moments in each other's arms.

We rarely hear about people happily in love, who commit crimes or abuse. I am convinced that if all the people in the world felt that they had enough food and security, there would be less demand for human trafficking. I also believe that if the entire population of the earth had received a good dose of love and empathy, the demand for human trafficking for commercial sexual exploitation would decrease significantly.

Being a dreamer, who longs for my next adventure, takes me on challenging inner and outer journeys and places I never thought I would visit, let alone call my "home". I want it all, and I want it now and am, therefore, part of the demand for human trafficking.

What? A criminal act, as in trading people?

Well, maybe not directly, but think about it. Across the world, people with limited choices work to produce the products we demand. Children in Pakistan may have made the t-shirt you are wearing and the carpet you stand on. The sugar on your pancakes might have been produced under poor working conditions in the Caribbean. Your children's toys may have been made in China. The fancy hotel in Dubai where you spend your vacation is probably built by migrant workers from Nepal or the Philippines. They are paid next to nothing for their skills and labour.

The scarcity principle

The word *economy* originates from Greek and means to manage with available resources. In the academic field of "economics", there are theories to explain the "economic man's behaviours" in a market.

The economic man has all the data and information needed to make the most intelligent opportunistic choices in any given situation. We, humans, who live on Planet Earth, tend to want to exchange things with each other (trade) and have sex (multiply ourselves) to pass on our genes whenever possible. Thereby driving us to exchange products or services for money.

The scarcity principle is an economic theory in which a limited supply of a product, coupled with-high demand for that product, results in a discrepancy between the desired equilibrium between supply and demand. According to the scarcity principle, the market equilibrium price occurs where the demand and supply curves meet. At this point, there are neither shortages nor surpluses for goods or services.

Of course, there are many internal and/or external factors that can cause the market to fall out of balance.

Consequently, the price for scarce goods or services will rise, until an equilibrium between supply and demand is reached. However, this could result in the limited supply of the goods only to those who can afford them. If the scarce resource happens to be grain, less affluent individuals will not have access to their basic needs.

This principle suggests that humans will consider a scarce commodity to have greater value than one in abundance. It thus creates a sense of urgency, and triggers consumers to act immediately before the commodity is no longer available.

Translating the scarcity principle to pornography

In economics, market equilibrium is achieved when supply equals demand. However, the markets are not always in equilibrium due to mismatched supply and demand levels in the economy. For example, when the supply of a commodity, let's say images of children's bodies for exploitation on porn sites, is greater than the demand for images of children's bodies, a surplus ensues, which drives the price down. Disequilibrium also occurs when demand for a commodity is higher than the supply of that commodity, leading to scarcity and, thus, higher prices for that product.

If the market price for images of children's naked bodies on the Internet goes down, for example, traffickers will be less inclined to maintain the equilibrium supply of pictures to the market, since the price may be too low to cover their marginal costs of production. In this case, traffickers will supply fewer children for the porn site owners to photograph, causing the quantity supplied to fall below the quantity demanded. In a free market, it is expected that the price will increase to the equilibrium price, as the scarcity of the product forces the price to go up.

When images of naked children are scarce, paedophile porn consumers are faced with conducting their own cost-benefit analysis, since a product in high demand but with low supply will likely be expensive. The consumer knows that the product is more likely to be expensive but, at the same time, is also aware of the satisfaction or benefit it offers. This means that a porn consumer will only purchase the product if he or she sees a greater benefit from having the product than paying the cost associated with obtaining it.

It is no news that marketers use the scarcity principle as a sales tactic to drive up demand and sales. The psychology behind the scarcity principle lies in social proof and commitment. Social proof is consistent with the belief that people judge a product as high quality if it is scarce, or if a lot of people appear to be buying it. On the principle of commitment, people who have committed themselves to acquire something will want it more if they find out they cannot have it. This is true for physical goods and services. It is also true for abstract phenomena such as satisfaction and happiness.

I have often been persuaded to start using a new product or service so as to reach another level of happiness. I hope to satisfy many basic needs when I change makeup brands or sign up for a new course online - "*because I am worth it*". I'll be more content when I, full of hope, completely refresh my old wardrobe with new items, just like the model in the picture, who seems to have everything - beauty, relaxed features and an aura of happiness. It is human nature to wish and to dream. Our need for touch and love is so deeply rooted in us that we cannot survive without it. When dating sites and pornography websites offer fake tenderness, affection and love through our computers, it is like dropping a potent sugar solution in our stimulation centres.

In Chapter 4, *How are you wired*? You will read about how our brain develops an addiction through its cravings for the glorious hormone, *dopamine.*

If we combine this knowledge with the economic theory about demand and supply and the scarcity principle, we can better understand the online sex industry.

Frequent porn consumption tends to escalate. Because of porn's addictive nature, porn consumers usually need an ever-increasing dosage over time, in order to feel the same level of enjoyment. As a result, they often have to seek out more extreme and hard-core forms of porn. Porn consumers can reach a point where they enjoy porn less and less, and yet, crave it more and more. This allows porn sites to strike gold, as consumers create greater and greater demand, without the producers getting any growing costs for marketing or sales. No cold calls are needed. No expensive advertisements. No time-consuming promotional campaigns. In addition, the industry's employees do not require as many resources from the HR department, if we are to incorporate business economics and profit returns into this discussion.

This is why pornographers who charge for their material can stay in business even if there is so much pornography out there, available at no cost.

In Chapter 10, you will read about PornHub. This is an interesting development in creating demand, which results in addiction and creates future paying clients. The scam is that they will enjoy it for free for a limited period, and later, when the charges are added, and there is nowhere else to go and get their fix, they will be hooked and start to pay.

Naturally, some customers will resist, but that's ok, because they will be caught later somewhere else in the big porn web. It will come as no surprise to you that this is supported by society and the music industry, which groom young people to be "porn ready". Many girls are still raised to be either fuckable or invisible. This is the norm we live by and, therefore sadly, society is unknowingly doing the grooming for the porn industry.

The founder of *Culture Reframed*, Gail Dines, has researched the pornography world and the sex industry for many years, and is one of the most knowledgeable researchers in her field. Please listen to her TED talk. It is as scary as it is brilliant and spot on[i].

Desensitisation

Just as there has been a normalisation of violence on film and in many TV series, the wide range of commercial sexual services on the Internet has driven us to become desensitised. This is yet another way our society plays its part in grooming young people on behalf of the sex industry. The advertising and marketing world is full of sexist messages and exploited bodies. It has become normal to sit a few inches from a photoshopped image of a half-naked model or bombarded with banners offering free live porn when opening your computer. What we know is that people in sexy clothing or sexual positions get people to look. Does this mean that consumers need more and more sex-based ads to respond?

This desensitisation could mean that the people who view pornographic images online over and over soon need more and more of their fix to get the desired effect. And yet again, demand goes up.

What was considered sexy in a 1930's film, or in the 1962 James Bond film that saw Ursula Andress emerge from the sea in a white bikini, will hardly satisfy anyone today.

I am not the one to tell people how to set their boundaries, but when young people are afraid of being called "*vanillas*" if they do not want to participate in "ass-to-mouth", strangling, or other forms of violent sex, something must be wrong.

It is time to start talking about intimacy and love and let boys express their feelings and vulnerability. What starts with society's expectations for young people to perform, can end with normalisation of acts of violence, and even trigger acts of rape.

The elements of Human Trafficking

When I first became involved in human slavery, I mainly thought of "*trafficking*" as a way to kidnap young people from a safe existence, and removing them to an unsafe place. This view is distorted, and highlights only a minimal part of the big problem. Human trafficking [ii]as a term includes three elements, the Act itself, the Means by which it is done, and the Purpose or reason it happens. Imagine a person who engages in so-called grooming on the Internet, ie. enticing someone else to perform an action. The Act itself can be to recruit, influence, bribe, or persuade someone to take nude photos, or to perform sexual services in exchange for payment or something else in return. The Means, the way in which it is implemented, can be by starting a chat with young people and pretending to be a friend but, in fact, being a perpetrator. The Purpose of why this happens is usually financial gain.

But of course, nothing is as clear cut as simply setting out the elements, as you will see as you explore this book, and hopefully take your reading beyond this content and information.

The impact

In reading this first Chapter, I hope you can see just how easily society has allowed these terrible things to happen. It only takes a moment for you to realise that you are being marketed to, and brainwashed, every second of the day.

Think about the last personal thing that you purchased. Got it? How did it come about? What about the perfume or aftershave that perhaps you purchased for your partner? The marketing of fragrances for men almost always plays on sex. A man with a bare torso, showing well-defined, hard muscles, stands above a woman with a seductive look and unleashed hair. Can you relate to this? First of all, I'm pretty sure that the scent does not turn every man into a sex bomb, and I'm completely convinced that a manufactured, unnatural smell will not drive women wild. In addition, the norm of a heterosexual couple is constantly repeated in the advertising we are exposed to, which only reflects part of the reality and desire in society.

You could argue that all PR is good. But the point is that many advertisers use sex to sell because it works. This means that you and I get used to seeing sexy things as the norm, and don't notice how it desensitises us. This is just another form of grooming, with the goal being the normalisation of objectification of human beings, especially women.

Now that I have your attention, I would ask that you continue to pay attention, and consider the impact this kind of marketing has on all young people in society. Especially those who are sold as consumable items due to trafficking. Imagine if those were your children. This thought can be hard to grasp, and if so, try to consider instead the impact this could have on their confidence and body image.

A recent example of how this is hijacking young people's brains is *OnlyFans*. For those of you who do not know what this is, let me enlighten you. Once there were girly mags like Playboy to titillate its readers, there is now a whole new stage available for budding pornstars to perform upon. Its popularity has grown quite simply because of the imposed lockdowns. People are looking at ways to make money, or to be entertained, without realising the inherent dangers.

This social media application, where you can start your private account, and upload content to attract followers, is an unpleasant attempt to manipulate mass grooming. PR tells you that you can become rich, famous and popular within a short period of time. So, influenced by this irresistible offer, you upload enticing material to your account, in order to attract followers who – you hope – will soon pay you a lot of money to see what you have to offer. I wonder how the app founders would react to their own child opening such an account, or discovering that they were being contacted by perpetrators pretending to be an 18-year-old admirer, asking for some innocent bathing pictures on the beach, or from the girl's room. Then, move on to asking the child to take slightly more daring pictures, "*because she is so incredibly sexy and good-looking*". What would the reaction be, when the founders of *OnlyFans* realise that the "*18-year-old admirer*" was, in fact, a horny 45-year-old who persuaded the child to come on a date? On this date, a rape takes place, and is filmed. Now, the 45-year-old has pictures that can be used as extortion if the child does not agree to meet other horny men, who are part of the demand for human trafficking. This reveals a large part of the real problem. If we want to make a significant and sustainable impact, we should focus on stopping the demand. This is, above all, a male issue. Although, as a man, you may be slighted by that comment. You may not recognise yourself in this description as a perpetrator and disgusting person. Would you dare to bring up the subject with your friends? Is it time to break the silence and make your voice heard? I hope you are a man who understands how uncool it is to buy sex. My dream is that you stand up, spread your word and break the silence. We need more like you.

Pause for thought

Now I'd like to invite you to pause for thought. This book is called the *Wall of Shame,* because shame is substantially embedded in the fabric of the sex trafficking industry and its economics.

We have all felt shame at some point, and this is when we feel that we have violated social and cultural norms. As a result, we will feel humiliated and see our whole self in a negative light. Shame is linked to guilt, and is usually where we feel guilt for an action, or set of actions.

One of the questions I have asked myself is, can shame be both healthy and toxic? Like all behaviour and emotions, shame has a broad spectrum. There is the healthy shame on one hand, which helps us understand the social norms in interactions with others. At the other end of the scale, we find the toxic shame, which hides in our subconscious bodies and pops up when we least expect it. This toxic shame can manifest itself in many ways, like a chronic sense of unworthiness, anger, blaming, addictive and/or compulsive behaviours, a sense of being punished, self-sabotage, indifference and low self-esteem. To admit to feeling ashamed takes courage, since we need to overcome all the feelings of unworthiness.

Just as shame is an emotion, the way in which we make choices is, in part, based on our emotions. You will have probably been taught about the apparent *"two halves"* of the one brain. One half is controlled by logic and the other by emotions. In reality, they work together all the time, but we'll each have our own individual preference because we are complex humans. This, of course, means that rarely will anyone make the same choices based on the same decision-making process, despite having access to the same information.

The same logic applies across all areas of life. When we consider the economics of supply and demand, these theories assume that we all have access to all the relevant information needed, to make rational economic decisions, in order to optimise our capital resources. They assume that we, as economic individuals, share the same preferences, and would make the same choice in every given situation.

But we don't all have access to good or verified data. It could be argued that economic data has probably become less reliable over time, despite the laws by which it is governed. Think about this: in a free market, anything can be sold if a willing buyer is found. This is used opportunistically and taken advantage of, by the very wealthy human trafficking industry. What intrigues me is how the sex industry contributes to each country's overall wealth, and how governments sit with the dilemma of building the economy and eliminating the greed and corruption in the human trafficking industry. Governments and economists alike would agree that selling a human being is not ethical – yet it continues.

When you add in poverty, which is one of the drivers of this industry, the game changes. One could argue that No one should ever need to buy a '*fuck*', have their penis sucked, or be able to masturbate to sex flicks. But poverty drives people into professions that they wouldn't, or couldn't, otherwise contemplate. And, of course, we know that many are driven to this against their will.

This is, of course, a grossly simplified picture of the world economy, but what I want to highlight here is the wall of shame I often encounter when meeting poor people, who can see no other alternative to selling their only asset: their bodies.

There are three main reasons why I started working against human trafficking at all. First, I was deeply touched by the shame I encountered in the people who were forced into prostitution. Their shame touched something inside me, like a projection that made me feel my own shame. Therefore, I could not let go of the questions these meetings raised. Second, I do it because I can. Third, I have the time and resources to spare to help in combatting human trafficking. Last, but not least, I am part of the demand that creates a trade with human beings. **<< in what way? Important to explain this statement** Who would I be if I gave this travesty my silent acceptance?

It would be wonderful to find a model country, we can call it Utopia, where everybody has access to food and clean water, somewhere to sleep, a home, someone to love and the ability to have children if they so wish. What if every human being could have the luxury of feeling economically and personally safe and healthy? We could also feel that we belong to a group that cares for one another and creates connections and bonds. Imagine a place where the goal was for all children to have good self-esteem, respectful behaviour, a belief that they can reach their full potential, become the best they can be, and the freedom to choose to be kind. Like Gandhi said: "*Be kind when possible. It is always possible.*"

Then we would be closer to the end of the demand for human trafficking. No demand equals no trade. Maybe artificial intelligence will be able to solve this equation in the future. In the meantime, let us do what we can to change the direction of the demand curve and challenge the scarcity principle, by appreciating what we have, rather than constantly wishing for more. I am working on feeling more grateful for the beautiful things and persons in my life. Are you?

Chapter 2

"We but mirror the world. All the tendencies present in the outer world are to be found in the world of our body. If we could change ourselves, the tendencies in the world would also change. As a man changes his own nature, so does the attitude of the world change towards him. This is the divine mystery supreme. A wonderful thing it is and the source of our happiness. We need not wait to see what others do."
Mahatma Gandhi

What Gandhi never said

In a yoga studio, I often visit, there is a quote from Gandhi. It says, "*Be the change you want to see in the world*". Perhaps this was his opinion, but he never said that. He actually said that change has to start from within before it can be expressed in the outer world. There's much more to what he said, but this has become my guiding star and philosophy.

Through life experience and spending time in different yoga communities, I have come to know that it is important to make the inner journey before I am able to feel confident in expressing myself and making a change. I notice that, as the changes I make are integrated, others react and have a different attitude towards me. This always fills my heart, because my desire is to bring kindness, grace and positivity to the world.

I love the quote, but wonder how it came to be changed to the extent that it has, to have had such a profound impact on the world. Gandhi's 1913 text actually says, *"We but mirror the world. All the tendencies present in the outer world are to be found in the world of our body. If we could change ourselves, the tendencies in the world would also change. As a man changes his own nature, so does the attitude of the world change towards him. This is the divine mystery supreme. A wonderful thing it is and the source of our happiness. We need not wait to see what others do."*

We mirror the world, and the world is a mirror for us. I wonder what you would like reflected back? We are all connected, and when we choose to change, we have the power and responsibility to create profound change around us.

What is important to me is that, while we want to do good, be good, be that person that others find inspirational, there is another side to all of us. Behind Gandhi's quote lies another side to him. I believe it's essential to address the terrible things that he *did* say.

'Terrible' and 'Gandhi' almost seem to repel each other when written in the same sentence, as if they are polar opposites. Unfortunately, this is not the case. Gandhi expressed some very important, peaceful, and positive sentiments. He was instrumental in the anti-colonial independence movement; however, the world is not black and white. While often touted as a 'good guy', Gandhi was known to say downright racist things - such as describing Africans as "*uncivilised savages*". I am telling you this because it is crucial to highlight the awful things figureheads have done alongside the wonderful. The bad does not water down the importance of his positive message. This is not to say I'm sweeping these actions under-the-rug, I just think it's increasingly important to acknowledge that our world is not made up solely of dichotomies. There is no such thing as 'good guys' and 'bad guys'; it is possible to be and do good while also having flaws (some greater than others). Gandhi's racism is unmistakable and inexcusable, though it does not mean we can't learn from his better, righteous pearls of wisdom.

Personally, I believe that no matter what has gone on in your life, it is more important that the **you,** who have learned and gained your own pearls of wisdom, show up now. That sounds so easy, doesn't it?

Imagine that you are sitting in a café and a friend or partner has just sent you a loving message; suddenly, you are awash with lovely thoughts and feelings. You look up grinning, and your expectation is that everyone around is feeling loved-up too, and will go on to be friendly and kind to each other. The truth is that they probably think you look a little strange. If you are lucky, you may catch someone's eye, and they will return the smile, and you feel like there is some kindness in the world. That they are on your wavelength and possibly share your values.

I believe that the essence of what Gandhi wanted to convey is that we need to find our own core values before trying to bring about a change in the world. And if we do not like what we see, change our own perspective on our own world, because it is impossible to change anyone else. The only thing we can do is to change ourselves and our attitude.

It's reflecting on quotes like this that leads to some compelling thoughts. One of which is releasing my judgement of others. This is important to me, given what I do. How can I stand in judgement of anyone, when I have no understanding of their life and what brought them to this point? Likewise, they have no idea how I came to be this beautifully complex creature I see in the mirror. It is seeing beyond the outer and into the inner beauty of others that stirs me into action and makes me want to lead by example.

You might ask why a quote from Mahatma Gandhi or Mohandas Karamchand Gandhi, his real name, was chosen. You may want to stop reading here, because it has been shared that Gandhi was not merely the saint that others claimed him to be. He was a wily operator and tactician, as well as being a charismatic leader, motivator and visionary, who had the ability to inspire his fellow human beings. He was a risk-taker, an extrovert and a creator. His peculiarities and flaws teach me something important; I cannot use my mistakes and shortcomings as excuses for not doing my best to change what I believe is wrong. And neither can you.

Another of my favourite leaders, the Dalai Lama, is also often quoted with, "If you want others to be happy, practice compassion. If you want to be happy, practice compassion."

Compassion is contagious. It is transformational. I think empathy is critical to the survival of the species. When we show empathy to others, we are creating a win-win for the evolution of the planet. One of the secrets to becoming happy doesn't just lie within yourself, but in your connection with others.

As I write this, the Corona Virus pandemic is in full flow. I'm acutely aware of how everyone around me is changing, no longer oblivious to others around them and showing incredible kindness. This tells me that most humans fundamentally thrive in a compassionate world. The world is quickly evolving, because it has to.

When I founded *Do Good Now Global*, I created a social initiative with the philosophy that you feel better when you are doing something for others. I wanted to invite everyone who wanted to participate, to contribute to this development. Everything happened subconsciously. The real thread through my life so far has been about having compassion for the vulnerable. Why? Because they are a reflection of myself, my shame and guilt over not being enough. I want to heal my inner, vulnerable child.

There is something profound inside of me that, like a raging forest fire, ignites my anger towards the predators who abuse other people. Or less deep, because I can? This is truly a paradox of life. These kinds of feelings will exist in you too. I think it takes a brave person to admit the very personal side of wanting to create change. But it is vital that we do. It is a part of who we are and forms the foundation of our core values.

I do indeed live a privileged life, which has made it easier to create *Do Good Now Global*. Thanks to the economic foundation my parents started building in the '50s, I did not have to depend on donations to make this happen. Thanks to Stefan (my husband), who loyally joins me from a distance on this journey, my hands are free to navigate this ship. Thanks to my inner exploration through therapy, healing, yoga teacher training, bodywork and meditation, I have become strong and flexible enough to create something beautiful. Thanks to my children, I understand the urgency for a more empathetic way to govern the world and steer the development towards more love, compassion and less greed.

It is because of the work with *Do Good Now Global* that I feel good. Through the connections, I can interact with awesome people, trips to faraway destinations and exotic places where I feel so alive and energised in my mission. My mission is not to change the world alone, because that is a false utopia and a practical impossibility. No, my plan is to build a tribe, and a community, who understand how good we feel when we show our greatness by being there for others – together.

But it has to start here. It has to start with me. Just as the change you want to create has to begin within you. While our paths may never cross or our values and ideals never meet, we are on a fantastic journey to, somehow, healing humanity. I am pleased to have you along for the trip.

This is all well and good, and you may be wondering why I am driven to all of this; why not simply enjoy the rewards of my success in another way? It's a great question when you consider that I have not grown up in the slums, I did not have an alcoholic parent, nor have I been subjected to any form of abuse as a child or as an adult. I am neither famous nor particularly good looking – which often bothers me, as it seems that this world is better suited to the beautiful, and to those who can attain celebrity status for whatever reason. This is, of course, my perception and judgement of the world. This serves to remind me that what I have instead is something even more valuable than beauty. I have the courage to step forward and declare that I will do whatever I can to make a change, to be the change and to support others who dream of a life that supports their values, dreams and desires.

When I look in the mirror, one part of me reflects the fear of not being beautiful enough. Another part of me feels good, because I can see my courage etched in my face. Naturally, there are traces of my vanity and the desire, like most women, for the next beauty product to reduce my lines. In the same mirror image, I see a woman who has the vision to change the world: one face and so many versions of it.

The truth is that most people don't care that you have the best foundation and lash extender, or that you have a few extra pounds; they care about your heart. As you apply your beauty and clothes, what if you look at them through different eyes? What if you asked conscious questions like, how much did it cost to get my products to me? Did anyone or any animal have to suffer before I could satisfy my ego? Rarely do we consider the bigger picture of how this world operates, when we chase the things that we think we have to have.

I can see that the Covid-19 pandemic has changed some of this, along with various campaigns and demonstrations around the slogan "*Black Lives Matter*". The greed that has overtaken us and pushed us into consumerism is changing. Have you noticed how the marketing message of "*We do not have enough? Make more products. Make more money. Buy more things*" is changing? The messages of consumerism are overwhelming. On the one hand, you have your core values, and on the other hand, you are bombarded and brainwashed with marketing messages.

I believe that there comes a time when we have to take action or be forced to do so. Everywhere I look, across all strata of society, I am confused. People with nothing give away their last possession to keep another person warm or fed. Many people share their wealth, but too many do not. Is it because they do not yet see the impact they could have on the world?

It is my wish and my hope that when I am 99 years old, I will look in the mirror and see a face where every wrinkle represents a victory for human rights. Therefore, I have to start with my own children and do everything I can to be a good role model for them. That's why I have to start with myself. How do I want to change, and why?

Before you read further, I would invite you to look up Gunhild Stordalen. She is wealthy and does incredible things for other people. You may have heard of her and her former husband, Petter Stordalen. You might argue, "*Yes, but it is easy for her because she has all the money she could ask for, and she does not have to make a sacrifice*". True, but she puts her money where her heart lies.

At the other end of the scale, you will have heard of Mother Teresa. Famous for her acts of kindness and compassion. What about Malala Yousafzai? She was shot in the head by the Taliban when she insisted on speaking out about girls and education in Pakistan. And Greta Thunberg will not have escaped your notice in her bid to raise awareness of climate change. And right now, you are getting to know me and what drives me to change the world. Add your name to this list of incredible humans. You may not know just yet what it is you have come to do, but it will become clear. I am delighted to meet you.

When you think about changing the world, what comes up? Hold that thought and let whatever it is come up. Notice it. When we feel fear, or imagine that we are an imposter, we can learn the most about ourselves. Perhaps you can hear the words *"who am I to…"*. You may have read the Marianne Williamson poem[iii], which has the line, "*who are you not to be*?"

Everything has to start with our core values. Before we can honestly go in the right direction, we need to know why we are doing things. Why, to me, seems like a primal force that I must follow. You know when your values are crossed, don't you? Often someone will have done or said something, an emotion arises, and you react. It's the way we are wired.

It took me a while to realise what my core values were. Sure, I knew I was feeling pain at what I saw in the world, and my heart hurt from the injustice. There was bewilderment in me at the cruelty that I witnessed. But things like justice did not resonate as a core value. There was something much deeper inside.

What are your core values? Do you know? It's quite fascinating when you discover them. Values are those things that tell you that your life is going in the right direction. The number that you have is not important, although I like to keep mine to three. What is important is that you know what they are, and why they are your values.

Cast your mind back over your life and career; when you started, were you motivated by success, then did you find that as your life changed, perhaps you valued more time with your loved ones? Maybe you found what makes your heart sing, your own stories? I can remember being curious about our family members, our place in the world, and how we interacted with the people around us and our environment. As a young child, I didn't see their passion. That would come later. Much later, I would come to understand how living a life with joy would be a massive driver.

Take a moment to connect to your heart and consider, without overthinking, what values you live by. When you think of your values, your core values, where do they show up for you? Ask why these are important to you, in relation to the direction your life is going and the things that you want to achieve? What does having these values give to you and others?

There is no meaning in knowing your values if you don't understand how they are an intrinsic factor in how you are wired. We'll talk more about how you are wired in Chapter 4.

My strongest values are curiosity, passion and adventure. Curiosity is a wonderful attribute if you allow it to flow. In some of my quiet inner child moments, I discovered a curiosity about my life's journey and what I have learned about life.

My lonely and introverted side spends a lot of time daydreaming and wishing – a treasure for the vivid imagination of an author. What started as a little child's craving for freedom, has resulted in a woman's battle against human trafficking.

Curiosity, and the desire to learn, have taken me to exotic places and given me opportunities to have meetings and conversations with inspiring people. My curiosity was intensified in southern Europe in the late eighties. The aim was to study French and Spanish. In Cannes, my curiosity about culture and language was birthed. I discovered that far away from home, I didn't need any filter, there were no judgements, and I could be my uncensored self.

Once my curiosity was awakened, I had to feed it further. Because of this, I have been around the world working on various projects, just as I have travelled extensively around my inner world.

This is a lovely quote from Albert Einstein *"I have no special talent, I am only passionately curious."* Einstein is known for his genius and for asking questions. If you ask and ask, it may annoy others, but the thing is that you will get to the root – you will get your answer. So keep asking.

It's curious, isn't it, this thing called curiosity? What exactly goes on in our brains when our curiosity is piqued? What happens to override everything, and for us to go on an adventure through our minds and lives? For me, it's an itch (my desire again) that needs to be scratched. I have to learn, understand and know how things work so that I can change the system (inner and outer) for good – if necessary.

Curiosity and passion are entwined, at least for me. I want to inspire and educate others to be curious. Passion is so misunderstood. In Chapter 13, we will explore this more.

Many times, the power of passion has grabbed hold of me and shown me the way. My passion for languages took me to England, France, Spain and Russia, from quite a young age to study, but the main reason was to meet new people from different cultures.

Far away from my home village, I could show whichever part of me I wished. Far away from the loneliness that drove me to hide and eat in the cupboards until I threw up, instead of daring to venture out, and let the world hear what I had to say. I have paid a high price for this, but there is far more that I have gained.

My first trip abroad without my parents was to attend a language course in Torquay, where I learnt to care for myself and solve problems as they occurred. I met my first real and deep love in France, a soulmate, who I hope lives according to his core values today. Russia was a unique adventure, which helped me better understand the soul of the Russian people, after so many years at war. In St. Petersburg, I understood the meaning of longing, as my boyfriend, who would later become my husband, was still based in Stockholm.

My passion for beautiful environments has given me the gift of experiencing what it is like to live in, experience, and understand many different aspects of some of the most beautiful places on Earth.

Passion guided me when I gave birth to our children, when I stubbornly struggled for visas in a bureaucratic maze, or when I convinced everyone in our family that we were all needed in a women's project in Costa Rica's jungle. Now!

And then there is adventure. Adventure takes me around the world to exotic places and fun-filled experiences with extraordinary meetings. Adventure is about exploring both my inner and outer worlds, and stretching myself beyond self-imposed limitations.

My education has taken me through a university degree programme, which was further enhanced by life experience. It was through my adventures that I discovered my passion for encouraging others to become curious and driven and, as a community, to rise together in a movement creating a new world, and supporting the ongoing evolution of Planet Earth.

Bringing adventure into my life has been fraught with challenges. There is the adventure of wonderful trips, and the compelling adventure inwards. The reward has been incredible clarity and awareness and knowing that, with transparency and honesty, I am making a difference.

Years ago, it was a different story. My well-hidden dream was to be a finely-sculpted ballerina, with strong muscles and a beautiful radiance. I longed to be on stage and be seen, listened to and validated. I wanted to travel the world on a dancing adventure, and to be part of something important, tell a story with captivating content and, above all, to count. To make a difference. Be empathic and to lead the dance with my heart.

I didn't escape to the ballet; instead, I found yoga and what an inner adventure that has been. It makes me strong in difficult times, and flexible when I need to adapt to new environments and situations. It helps me to show vulnerability without shame or guilt.

Through my values of curiosity, passion and adventure, it is my mission to be as humble and graceful as possible, towards both my outside world and to myself. I believe this is what Gandhi's quote is all about. I believe this is the highway to harmony and peace.

Now you know a bit about my world and what drives me. What about you? Which are your core values? What do they mean to you? May I suggest you read these quotes from changemakers I admire, and imagine their beliefs? If you want, reflect on how they sit with your values? What do you feel motivated to do?

"It is not beyond our power to create a world in which all children have access to a good education. Those who do not believe this have small imaginations." Nelson Mandela

"Many investors still think impact is a sector-based investment. They don't understand that impact is about creating change, and that all businesses need to have a purpose. From now on, the climate issue needs to be ingrained in every decision making on every level of society." Ingemar Rentzhog

"Change will not come if we wait for some other person or if we wait for some other time. We are the ones we've been waiting for. We are the change that we seek." Barack Obama

"I have learned you are never too small to make a difference." Greta Thunberg

Are you questioning your values – the ones that really mean something, and which you use to shape your world? Your values bring you back to who you are, what you want and how you live.

Is there a time you remember when you made a choice, in alignment with your own vision, of how you would like to show up among others?

Can you recall when was the last time you used your voice for or against something, about which you have strong convictions?

Consider what your life might be like if you didn't live by your values. What if no-one had any values? What kind of judgments would be made? What would slip through the net of decency? The impact is almost too shocking to consider.

Chapter 3

"Of the total of 15.4 million forced marriages that took place in 2016, 5.7 million were children, the majority of whom were girls." ILO *"global estimates of modern slavery 2017,* UNICEF *"facts about child marriage."*

Belonging

Sometimes I wonder where I belong. Do I belong to my family, or to the tribes of individuals whose conditions I want to change? Of course, I belong to both. They are part of who I am and who I will become. Belonging also makes me feel about how I belong to myself and in my body. My body is my home, it's where I live, and it's the gift I received when I was born.

The knowledge that I was a long-awaited daughter has always been within me. After ten years of my parents' waiting, longing and dreaming of a child, I knocked on their door, or rather on my mother's pelvic floor. The bleeding was intense and almost resulted in a miscarriage. It happened twice. But the Universe had other plans for us. My parents had already booked flight tickets to Korea, to meet and hold their adopted daughter, when I made my entrance into the world and turned theirs upside down. I cannot imagine the sorrow they must have felt, while burning the photo of the little Korean girl, their daughter-to-be, and my sister, who I never got to know. I took her place and the role of completing my parent's lives. I often wonder how she is?

I was treated like porcelain. From my pedestal, I believed I could achieve anything by dreaming it, and get anything if only I wished hard enough. And so I wished all the time. I did not understand; I had to speak it out. I never said I wanted to be a performer; I kept my secret well hidden and worked hard for my school grades. I belonged to a hard-working, entrepreneurial community, whose goal was to climb the status ladder. It is in our DNA to try to fit into the tribe, so I chose to study business administration, economics and finance, and put my performing dreams in a golden cage. Does that seem pretentious? Possibly. That is part of how I am. This is the privilege and the shortcoming of a spoiled brat. Sometimes I mix my endeavours up with who I AM. This is where it becomes complicated, like really complicated. Having reasonable confidence by doing, or grounded self-esteem by being, are completely different epithets. You can struggle for a lifetime, trying to find your life purpose – but first, you need to know where you belong.

My wonderful mum would do anything for anyone, and would bring down the moon for me if I asked her. She looked perfect to me and, as I observed her dressing up or putting her makeup on, I figured I also needed to perform the role of her perfect image. Thus, *'perfect'* equalled slim, ambitious and utterly decent. These qualities are light-years from my nature, which is characterised by impulsivity and disorder, mixed with a portion of chaos. Mum was always kind and loving and never raised her voice to me. Our relationship was close to a symbiosis. She was raised as an only child, with no siblings with whom to challenge or explore her boundaries. Of course, she and I became one in her world. This unity is lovely to experience as a toddler but less enjoyable as a teenager. My mother did not want to set boundaries. On the other hand, I had a great desire to push my limits and explore beyond what I could see.

Still, my ideal image was to be slim like her, a petite ballerina. But this is not me, and it never was. My mum is tiny and delicate, stunningly hair-styled and impeccably dressed at parties. While my natural inclination was to become the polar opposite for a while, I tried to be a punk rocker, and I was desperate to look like Robert Smith. If I couldn't push the boundaries with my relationships, I tried to do it with my looks. I wanted to be different and to break the mould of a family of beautiful women.

I wanted to reject my body, upbringing, society, how I should be, look and act. It was as if the very purpose of belonging was to not belong. I didn't know how to practice living inside my body, so I found it tricky to practice living with my family and those around me.

While I confused everyone else with my looks, they left me to it. The test I'd set for my family failed. They loved and accepted me, which tipped me even further into a hole. I filled this hole with food. It was freely available, and the more I stuffed my face, the more I wanted to. All I ever seemed to do was push boundaries, and no-one cared.

Belonging is such an essential human need. Not just to belong, but to be accepted as one of the team. I have often felt that my belonging to my family group was like being raised in a mafia, but without the drugs and weapons, or maybe like a cult without the overt brainwashing. You might even call it tribal. Tribes care for, cultivate and tend the needs of the members.

This fantastic group was full of strong individualists – independent women or children who were not part of it unless you were married or born into it. It was, and still is, very loving and caring. And it was because I was part of this strong dynamic that I learned to rely on the group, and only the group.

I imagine that there are many families like this. Close-knit and entangled in each other's affairs. Where everyone, like in a clan, has a role to play, and where it helps to create a purpose in their lives.

In our clan, the oldest male holds the power – he is like a Godfather. I learned early on that the head male sets the codes of conduct and informal rules within our family. What he believes to be the values of the clan are also our values. Not everyone agrees, of course, and lots of jokes have been made around this. I know that some of the jokes mask a serious underlying reason, but I'm not sure exactly what that reason is.

My understanding is that there are rules enabling us to keep the family whole and united. One of the greatest things about our family is that we know that we belong together, and can all call on each other for help. Yet, despite all of this belonging, there has always been a longing for freedom and to explore what it might be like to not belong. Perhaps seeking a different kind of connection. For whatever reason, I felt that something was missing, or that it was part of my purpose to test what 'belongingness' meant to me instead, and simply to accept that this is simply the way it is in my family.

What I found curious, in my bid to test the boundaries of the group rules, was how secrets were handled. As with all families, there are secrets. What piqued my curiosity was that the family had rules, and we showed a united front in abiding by those rules. Ironically it was often the ones who set the rules who broke them. It was they who held the secrets. And yet, despite the secrets, we maintained our united front.

One of the things that I didn't realise until much later, because I didn't understand what was going on, was that our family helped rebuild society after the war – creating support systems and being a part of the power base for restoration. Imagine that, wanting to escape and test everyone, thinking that they were trying to brick me in when, in reality, they were breaking down walls.

My father was a street smart, innovative business person with humanitarian values. I remember that he insisted that his staff should all own a small part of the company. In hindsight, I can see that he was altruistic. He must be the one from whom I got my passion and drive to fight injustice. He also taught me how to put money to good use, which is how I am able to use what I have for the greater good.

My father wanted to give me a solid economic foundation. He succeeded. My mother wanted what my father wanted. I believe she is what many men would call the 'dream wife'. Beautiful, never complaining, happily smiling, the ideal hostess for holding presentation dinners and events with customers, which we often held in our home since my father is so proud of his family. I think he really appreciated and admired her as well, in her attempts to please him.

Sometimes I feel that she was clearly subordinate, but greatly loved, as are most women in our family. It's how, I guess, families who have a patriarchal structure, with three generations of men and boys, fathers and brothers, are functioning.

Back then, I couldn't see any of this. All I saw was a tight-knit family that wasn't going to let outsiders in. It was with these perceptions and ingrained values that I cruised through life. So that, when I met my husband, who already had two children, I was confident that they didn't need me or that I would have any role in their lives. Surely they had their own clan or tribe to look after their needs. They already had a mother. Why would they need another? Later I learned that this was unacceptable thinking. We should never ignore children when they move into our lives.

Despite the tightness of the clan, my deepest fear was the feeling of loneliness. I didn't consciously choose to be lonely or alone, yet I did, and I was. So much so that wherever I went, I wanted my group, my great family, with me. They kept me safe, and I felt protected by their rules. The unwritten rules of the clan are ingrained in me: never leave your clan; do not mix with strangers; blood is thicker than water…

Yet, I felt different, and despite going out of my way to be different and to discover where I belonged, I fitted in, where I could. There was often a sense that I belonged with my family, yet I didn't want to be with them or perhaps the country we were in. Or that I loved being with them, yet I yearned to do my own work, to follow my own passion.

In the murky depths, I think that I always needed an audience, and the best place to find one was with my family, even if I sometimes rejected their warmth. My husband gave me a stage, just as my parents had done, which somehow seems both convenient and cowardly. I never thought anyone from the outside world would praise my endeavours. By playing to my closest audience, I could make it sound more courageous and more creative than the truth would reveal.

Being the jewel in the crown and the much-wanted child, as you can imagine, made me very precious and, as I was to discover, this came with a lot of pressure. As an outsider looking in, you would only see a perfect life, and it seemed I could be and do anything because I was loved, but I often wondered what I *should* do? Imagine that! Having complete free reign to do anything, and that anything was possible, and yet I didn't know what to do with myself or for the world, let alone knowing where I could do great things?

It seemed to me that at all times of the day, there were eyes on me. As I was raised higher onto a pedestal, it appeared that there were no boundaries or anyone to guide me into sound integrity. To ease this confusion, I tried to fill my emptiness with food. Emotional eating is a strange bedfellow. I loved food, but I had found myself inexplicably alternating between not eating and overeating, and occasionally vomiting. There was also that feeling of not being happy but not knowing why. On reflection, there was a perceived constant pressure to be happy and pretty.

When what you observe around you are people who seem to be happy and living their perfect lives, you tend to feel disconnected and out on a limb, yet somehow also a part of it all. What I have experienced is a conflict within myself that could only ever end in disaster. Not a visible disaster, as in some of the places I have been to lend my support, more of a failure in terms of emotional eating and hankering after 'freedom'. So much so that I have fought the systems and structures that surround me, while simultaneously allowing them to hold me.

I know that we are 'feeling bodies' that think. We feel first and then think, yet it seems that this natural way is sometimes overridden. We dip into avoidance, numbing ourselves and judging others. It's been during my time on the yoga mat that I have learned that connection to ourselves is truly being connected to our feelings, and this is where belonging starts. I've learned to face my emotions, judgements and numbing behaviours. It's seeing into my soul that has helped me to understand not only my own family, and the families I seek to support, but also those who behave in despicable ways. We all only ever want to belong.

I have found that powerful experiences emerge when I am connected to my purpose, values, and beliefs. Understanding and being connected to my curiosity has motivated and inspired me to get out of bed every day. It's my own values that guide me and bring me back to my centre, and to the place that I truly belong. It is from the core of my being that I am free to follow my passion and indulge in adventure.

It is interesting how belonging can direct your life. My heart loves freedom. My way out has never been unfaithfulness or suicide, but in escaping to far-away places. It was also a way that I felt empowered to break with my emotional eating. It is not a coincidence that our first family adventure happened in Australia – the other side of the world from Sweden.

Australia seemed like a long way to go to break away from the perceived chains of the clan and my inner demons. No-one said that this would be easy, and nor was it. But it was just the adventure I needed on my way to discover and realise my passion.

It is well-known that many people wanting to 'escape', will choose Australia. So did we. The Swede, who was never to be my husband, put a ring on my finger on a beautiful day in December 1996. We spent a month-long honeymoon backpacking in – yes – in Australia.

Six years later, we filled a container with clothes, bicycles, things we didn't think we could do without, filled in the customs declaration and booked tickets to Sydney. This time to stay for a year, during our parental leave. What made us leave everything for a while was simply an urge to start over. We ran two companies, had two little girls, with whom, in line with our own values, we didn't spend enough time. I remember the sadness in my father's eyes when we announced that we no longer wanted to be part of the family business. We turned our backs on everything he and mum had worked for, since the day they married. Now, almost twenty years later, with four children, of whom two are young adults, I can feel the pain Daddy's eyes radiated. "*Together forever, all for one and one for all*", no longer applied.

My father first asked me, "*And what the hell are you going to do there?!*" The question lingered in the air for a while, until the feelings of shame enveloped me. Yes – the question was relevant. We had been given a beautiful beachfront house with a jetty. What would we do in Australia?

While I heard a malicious inner voice whispering disaster, I heard myself thinking that I would write articles for a newspaper and work with x and y studies... While delivering the lies one by one so that I believed myself, I kept the truth hidden deep inside. I wanted to get back to basics with ourselves and our little family, without demands and control. It was as simple as that. Now, in retrospect, I am able to recognise this for what it was. But then, 20 years ago, it was impossible for me to speak.

My father turned to my husband, who was more courageous and, unlike me, quite open and honest. "*I'm not going to do anything*," he said. I wanted to sink through the floor and never resurface. I was now a cheater who had betrayed the family's code of conduct.

So what did we learn during our sojourn in Australia? That Australian people, in general, are very generous and helpful, laid back and responsible in a very balanced combination. We now understand how isolated Australia is from the rest of the world, geographically and news-wise. If Australia holds a presidential election, or if the bush fires threaten the entire New South Wales, no-one outside Australia really knows or cares. We learnt that the Aboriginal people are side-lined, judged and excluded, and live quite a miserable life, often in the struggle and turmoil of drug addiction and poverty. Most importantly, we learnt how to build and nurture a stronger bond of belonging within our own family. Looking back, our Australian adventure was part of the red thread in my life, wanting to ensure that my children were given the opportunity to live a life with passion and curiosity. We also learned that you do not need much to live a comfortable life, that parks are undervalued, and outdoor living makes you happy. When watching the whales swimming by from our elegant and worn patio, we forgot about the fact that we rented, without any doubt, the ugliest house in the street. I can still feel the wooden planks, heated by the sun, against my body as the whole family lay sunbathing in our 'eagle's nest'. Our parental leave abroad taught us that the time you spend with your children is worth more than all the gold in the world — hopefully for the children and especially for yourself.

The more I have become connected to myself, the more I have gained the confidence to share my vulnerability with the world. I am certainly doing that by writing a book. My connected self can set better boundaries, though not all of the time. This means taking responsibility for my actions and emotions. This also means that the better I understand myself, the better equipped I am for the exploration ahead. Because in this journey, I have to share myself with kindness, compassion and strength.

Thanks to my innate curiosity, I know where I belong, and that I can stand alone in the wilderness of oppression against others, and be a voice for them. Through curiosity, I can slay my own demons, lose my fear of loneliness, build a community and support others to trust in connection and belonging.

I want to leave you with these thoughts.

Who you are is a direct result of who you were born to, where you have come from and the influences and lessons that life delivers. It's worth taking a moment to reflect back on your life and ask, '*how was I made?*'

This brings to mind the story of Pinocchio, which always confused me as a child. Why couldn't he just become a boy? Now, with my own life experience, I have more clarity on the meaning behind the story.

This is not to suggest that you are like Pinocchio, or that you were carved from a piece of wood. But imagine for a moment that your parents were like the inventor who created the wooden boy. They would have wished (in my case) for a child, and they would, from the depths of their hearts, have wanted their child to be born healthy and to have a good life – the one that they could provide, with all of their resources, skills, knowledge and wisdom.

In the film, Gepetto creates a wooden boy, who is given life by the Blue Fairy. He, like your parents, has a real child in front of him, and no manual for what to do next. For Pinocchio, his role in life is simple...

"Prove yourself brave, truthful, and unselfish, and someday, you will be a real boy," says The Blue Fairy to Pinocchio.

From this point on, he has to learn from his experiences, making many mistakes on the way to becoming a real boy. Later, risking his life to save his father, Pinocchio is granted the wish of becoming a real boy.

If only it were so simple. However, this might be a perfect time to reflect on your roots, your entry into this world and your own sense of belonging.

The impact

Travelling with a curious mind has helped me to understand what belonging means to me. I had to go far away to come home, to find my space in the world and within myself. With this internal base, I founded ***Do Good Now*** with the ambition to influence someone positively, wherever I am in the world.

What feelings are evoked within you when you read about belonging? What does it mean for you to belong? Do you think that it means that being a part of a group or a community is a fundamental part of being human, or is it something else?

When and where do you feel like you belong in this world? These are great thought-provoking questions, aren't they?

Whether it's a child bride or a young girl, or a boy forced into prostitution, being sold or snatched out of context must totally destroy all sense of belonging. On one hand, you have a home and, on the other, when faced with the chance of freedom, you may find yourself homeless.

Envision what it must feel like to be forced into a community where all freedoms are removed. This means freedom of movement as well as freedom and control of your own mind, body and spirit. Perhaps the only freedom that endures is your curious mind, which allows you to wonder how you will endure another day in hell, and what it would feel like to be truly liberated and in a place where you feel safe and loved.

One has to question how children, who already lack a sense of belonging and inclusion, are affected by this entrapment? They likely feel lonely, deep sadness and wonder what is wrong with them, along with their inherent feelings of abandonment and rejection.

As we know, it is a basic need for children to belong, have a safe place, and be validated and cherished. Most likely, they will look for a context where they can be counted and given a role of usefulness and relevance. So they will try to fit in where they don't belong, or become a people pleaser. They may roam from place to place, from person to person, never finding inner peace. These people most often have a sense of yearning that follows them for the rest of their lives. What we don't want is for them to attach themselves to people who will continue to abuse them, while continuing to manipulate their freedom and brainwashing them into thinking that they belong.

Again, I think a lot of this rests on the shoulders of our boys, supported by parents who are good role models. If we want our boys to think it is cool to be kind and caring, they need role models who treat women with respect and dare to talk about their feelings. The boys and girls who will be the new leaders in our society are those who understand the concept of empathy and compassion for others. Something has to change to create healthy communities where people don't numb themselves with food or substances, or remain caught up in unhealthy, abusive situations.

A sense of belonging is important in our diverse culture. No matter where someone comes from, their background or experiences, everyone deserves inclusion and respect. By giving our children a safe and supportive space, they can blossom into global citizens who will go on to create a safer world.

The bottom line is that we all belong. By being aware of what trafficking does to essential freedoms, I hope the impact will be more informed people, working towards creating less demand for human trafficking. I'll leave you with this question: *if a man is equipped with healthy values and good self-esteem, why would he want to buy sex or rape someone*?

Chapter 4

"Frequent porn consumption tends to escalate. Because of porn's addictive nature, porn consumers usually need an ever-increasing dosage in order to feel the same level of enjoyment, and they often have to seek out more extreme and hard-core forms of porn. Porn consumers can reach a point where they enjoy porn less and less, but want it more and more." Fight The New Drug [iv]-

How are you wired?

I never wake up entirely happy. There's always a feeling of having a trillion tasks to finish before I can sit down with a cup of tea. I have to win even the most straightforward game, to prove myself 'worthy'. I compete with everyone, including myself. No wonder many of my friendships don't last.

When someone knows me too well, and I can no longer hide behind my alter ego, I feel the urge to escape. What if they find out that I am nothing, that I am just pretending? The shame is always on my doorstep, waiting to enter when I lose, because I am convinced that I will. The guilt of not being enough, whether inherited or self-developed, is present in everything I do. I think others see me as the stubborn one who never gives up, who keeps reaching for the moon when the sun rises. That description of a thick-skinned fighter is not true. The fact is, I am determined to never stop fighting for those with no voice. Because if I stop, I think I will disappear.

This might sound depressing or strange to you. Or perhaps it resonates, and you can empathise? There is an upside to everything, and mine is that I am continually aiming to improve my performance. My self-worth is measured in how wisely I invest, how hard I work and how fit my body is. Reaching a goal is never enough for me, because being in the process of working towards something 'bigger' is my comfort zone. Unconsciously, I am drawn to people who motivate me to do better – my children, my personal trainer, my yoga instructor, my co-workers, my therapist, my publisher. They see something in me and search for my highest qualities, all of which motivates me to be my best self.

Seeking to stop the demand for human trafficking for commercial sexual exploitation is the perfect challenge. I've looked at the characteristics needed: I must be smart, hard-working, able to compete under time constraints, and prepared to influence and convince the world that we need a paradigm shift. Not only that, I need to be able to creatively construct ways to make the shift towards more humane treatment of each other, and provide education to all children in the world. I realise that education for *all children* is a lofty goal; however, it is my dream. The reality is that I can want this with all of my being, but as with all things in life, doing it requires something different from myself.

Visionaries and dreamers need hands-on, structured and organisational people to help manifest their ideas — people who can bring order out of chaos. I have clear visions but lack excellent communication skills. That seems like a bad combination. In addition, there is my fear of letting go and handing over essential roles to others. Because I want to be the leading lady, the admired one on the stage. The other side of the coin is loneliness. Why is being an adult so tricky at times? Can someone please just put me back on the pedestal and respect me for who I am, not just for what I do? I want to take the ballerina skirt off, step down off my stage, and use my voice for those who have had their opinions stolen by poverty, oppression, and slavery.

Now that I have heard their stories, who am I to let them down? I can't let them down; they are a part of me now — a part of my heart and a part of my life. I am still wondering where I can find my stage. Like the girls in the porn movies, I am like those girls who strive for better poses, obeying the producers and filmmakers, to deliver better orgasms.

When I stand back and consider the doing and the being, I know that now their stories and experiences are mine too. I have to win something for them. It is about winning. This is no longer playing.

I learned about winning from my family. Every midsummer, the whole family gathered together. This gathering was the highlight of the year, when siblings, cousins, grandparents, aunts and uncles met to enjoy the summer, hang out and have fun together.

I can still hear the sound of tyres on gravel as we turned off onto the smaller road that meant it was just a few kilometres through the woods and fields, until we could see the roof of my aunt and uncle's immaculate house, next to the glittering bay. Memories of joy and happiness filled me and made me laugh out loud. I knew that the following days would be filled with rides on quad bikes, windsurfing and fishing with the adventurous boys next door, who seemed to have come to life from my idyllic children's books. But they were real children, and I was lucky enough to meet them. Not to mention their older sisters. The most beautiful girls I had ever seen. At their place, it was so indulgent. We were allowed to sit in their messy and homely kitchen, drinking tea and talking all night. In that kitchen, my dream of a large, bohemian family was born.

As we approached my aunt and uncle's place on the east coast archipelago, you could feel that the atmosphere in the car was changing. Either it had to do with my mother's way of retouching her lipstick, or the tone my parents used as they talked to each other. I could not put my finger on exactly what was different, but there was both excitement and expectation in the air. I cranked down the car window and savoured the scent of pine forest and sea. We drove past fields and pastures. A cow looked curiously up from her rambling and held me with her gaze, as if she wanted to make sure everything was alright.

As the car pulled to a stop, I could see my aunt through the kitchen window, preparing the traditional midsummer buffet. This was like waving a red blanket in front of a bull. Eating would have been a simple thing if I had kept my promise to lose those five kilos. On the contrary, I had lost that fight with myself, and the food would, therefore, be my challenge this weekend. I had brought two dresses. The one in case I was feeling slim at dinner time. The other if I felt, as usual that is, five kilos too fat. My brain immediately started working, trying to find the best strategy for the buffet challenge. I allowed myself to have all the fish dishes but no carbohydrates like bread and potatoes. Strawberries were permitted, without the cream, of course. The potato gratin was just to be forgotten, as were the candy bowls and the cheese platters. If a green salad were served, I would build a mountain as a base under the rest of the food. Nobody would notice my game of finding the combination of the least possible number of calories. Good plan. Good girl.

My thoughts were interrupted by the deafening sound of my father, loudly blowing the horn to announce our arrival. Two of my cousins immediately stopped their activity of pulling chairs and tables across the courtyard. A loud laugh was heard when the car was parked, and the car door flew open. There he was, my lovely funny cousin, with the guitar over his shoulder. Always ready to entertain us younger cousins. A middle ground between siblings' love and friendship. Our bloodline.

The show could begin. You can imagine, with so many people, that we had many planned activities to entertain us. The list included picking flowers and dancing around the midsummer pole, laughter, the adults drinking schnaps, to the accompaniment of drinking songs. Nobody got too drunk, as I recall. The joy was the focus, as well as the hugging. We were physically surrounded, often walked and held each other while playing or conversing. No-one ever crossed the line, or made anyone feel uncomfortable, as I remember it. Hugs were part of our way, inherited from our grandmother, who loved giving tender and sweet kisses. Until the end of her life, she wanted to deliver kisses, even to the nursing home staff! She was something of an original. Growing up and, for most of her childhood, commuting between Denmark and Sweden, with aunts who gave her whatever she wished for, but without a present mother. She is the one who began to tie all the friendship threads in our family. Probably because she lacked strong family bonds herself. Maybe because that was just the way she was. Passionate and loving.

When the adults were caught up in grown-up-talking, the younger ones would head for the sauna, and then dive into the sea to cool off their steaming bodies in the soft summer twilight.

Some of us would fall victim to one of the many warm-hearted, practical jokes that were part of the ritual. Someone was pushed into the water from the dock, with all their clothes on. Someone else had a tough ride in the water-skiing. We, the children, could stay up as long as we wanted, and we played hide-and-seek barefoot in the dewy grass.

It is only in recent years that I have analysed our gatherings at a deeper level. There was one particular moment during our family celebrations that I loved. In retrospect, I've been wondering why. It usually had to do with witnessing my dad win something. My instinctive role was to be the shy girl among very dear, but tough and extroverted, boy cousins, who also wanted to win.

One significant event that played out was our big outdoor pentathlon. Everyone was divided into three teams. Naturally, the team leaders were my father and his two younger brothers.

The competition consisted of mostly athletic themes, which required either physical strength or skills for ball sports. Which all ended with a clothing relay.

Since my dad was the leader and physically the strongest, he chose the most competitive team players and, of course, his team won by far almost every time. It had a very positive effect on his mood, which was crucial for the continued party atmosphere.

A few things come to mind. Playing means competing. Success is synonymous with winning. Winning is addictive, and addiction is fed by dopamine – the so-called pleasure neurotransmitter.

This leads me to wonder how far dopamine is helping me to seek pleasure and reward as I look for ways to win, and how much of the polar opposite effect it may have on me, in my drive to succeed. So that my winning becomes an almost compulsive behaviour. I feel that I have to win, in order to survive in the jungle around me.

I am the worrying kind, still searching for my place in this world. Like U2, I still haven't found what I'm looking for. Until then, I keep competing. I compete with the scale, and the former, present and future versions of myself.

When I fast forward my life today, I can see that everyone is competing for survival. Survival is the premise of Maslow's hierarchy. Our root chakra needs to be balanced for survival in the chakra system, and for creating strong roots from which to grow

In our essence, we all want to be safe and secure. This includes our basic needs such as food, water, shelter, safety, as well as our emotional needs of interconnection and belonging. When these needs are met, we feel grounded and safe. When we are at odds with these needs, life can spiral out of control, and we can often feel overwhelmed by our thoughts, leading to feelings of lack of groundedness and connection.

It is clear that we learn a lot about this from our parents. What they do and how they do it, is imprinted in our minds. As a child, you have little reason to doubt how your parents behave, what they say or how they treat others. After all, they are the ones who provide you with safety and security. They did the very best they could with the resources that they had.

And therein lies a problem.

These end up being 'mini-scripts' in your brain, and each time you witness one, it builds a more prominent groove in your brain. These are your neural pathways. In our heads is the wiring of years of conversations and experiences that have all played a part in shaping our perceptions of ourselves. From early on, we learn how to survive in a world that makes little sense to us.

Perhaps you can remember times where you met your parent's eyes, and they only reflected disappointment. Basically, you are not enough. Whatever the perceived failure, we register a view of ourselves that has been given to us by someone else.

The feeling of not being good enough hurts, and when it hurts enough, you will eventually find a way to numb the pain. When I look back at those long summers, and the shame I felt when not being on the winning team, I can see clearly how I came to choose food as the way to numb my pain.

My neural pathways were always full of food, in a futile attempt to numb my guilt, shame and internal chatter. My script would tell me to escape and take me into a world where there was only me – and the carbohydrates. In my mind, there are soft marshmallows, just waiting to be swallowed quickly, with smooth vanilla ice cream that just wants to melt in my mouth, along with whipped cream oozing a delicious, fluffy texture. All that was there to 'comfort' me, like a tender hug.

I have this image of myself, with nothing to do, my mobile turned off, and only the sound of my chewing and swallowing, chewing and swallowing, chewing and swallowing... like a soothing mantra. Everything's alright, everything's alright, everything's alright. Only me and my fix. This never used to leave me.

My brain is my best friend and my worst enemy. It allows me to indulge in all of the experiences and emotions that life has to offer, cry when a dear one is hurt and, as I realise, it quickly traps me into addictions. I have so many opportunities in the world and yet, I still often choose to fall for the emotional eating monster.

Could I have taken drugs to escape? What about sex or some other addiction? No, I knew that they would never have worked because I already had the perfect drug. Food, shame and my emotions. I've argued endlessly with myself. Look how happy I am. I have children, I can travel, and I have projects. So why can't I be the perfect weight and eat what I want?

The battle never ends. I want to be a voice for people who have no voice, yet I cannot quieten the one that makes ridiculous demands from me. It seems that I am more in control when I am following my passion. But like a sober alcoholic, sometimes I fall back into the trap. When that happens, I know I have great tools - yoga, meditation and rest. Sometimes my deep inhale wins over the temptations of the fridge.

My conclusion is that I am in a continual cycle of being happy with my doing, and not my being, and then not satisfied with my doing, and feeling worse about my being, and then returning through my adventures to being happy with my doing.

It's through my search for answers to emotional eating that I make a discovery about brain chemistry and other addictions. I also discovered that the people I want to help – the girls who have been sexually abused – are more likely to have a food or drug addiction. I presume that they, like me, are filling the holes in their lives with something to dull the pain and the ache for love and belonging. It is strange to think that it doesn't matter where you come from, or how you were brought up, how privileged or not, we can all be held to ransom by the giant that is the brain.

Our emotional brains strive for control. Humans are driven by necessities such as food, sleep, procreation, no pain, feeling safe, and reward. It turns out that my battles are, in part, to do with dopamine, the motivation and reward chemical, the neurotransmitter in our brains. It signals the brain to say, hey, wake up; you are about to feel good. We all like to feel rewarded so that we stay motivated to continue doing whatever it is that makes us feel alive. Dopamine helps you to remember this feel-good factor, so that you want to do it again.

In my case, it pushed me towards my friend, the fridge. Then I would compensate with exercise. I became an addict. I couldn't stop my enslavement to food, nor halt the shame, which led to my addiction to exercise. I can assume that it is similar for anybody who is a slave of any addiction.

I think of myself being a part-time slave to addiction; anyone who has ever found themselves craving something, feeling out of control and doing whatever it is regardless, will understand. I believe that this is similar for porn addiction.

The addict will demand more and more to get the same arousal sensation. Am I like a porn addict who believes that they cannot change? The more I learn, the more I need to know. I need answers. Answers for me, and solutions for the girls I want to help.

This search for answers has taken me on a fascinating journey. When researching the way porn addicts operate, I learned that shame lies at the root. Like I used food to numb myself, and over-exercising to compensate for the shame, an addict does the same. I had a process whereby I'd end up in the fridge, stuffing my face. I guess a porn addict would find themselves cruising the internet for their fix.

In 2014 scientists conducted research into which areas of the brain were activated when someone is addicted to porn. Three parts of the brain, including the amygdala, were activated in the same way that drug addicts are affected.

How you respond within the first few seconds after encountering that sexually provocative image makes all the difference. Get away from it as fast as you can, and you have a fighter's chance to repel the hijackers. Linger on that image, and the sexually-charged "fight or flight" part of your brain will assume control and the rational brain checks out.

Compounding this effect, the "good thinking" part of the brain – the prefrontal cortex – goes offline. Precisely what happens when I fall for that chocolate bar or ice cream. For a milli-second, we might think about how too much food (drugs, alcohol, cigarettes or porn) has ruined parts of our lives, including perhaps our job. Just a tiny bit of temptation blocks out your wise and perceptive prefrontal cortex, and you are thrown back into your comfort zone, ie. your addiction.

I am very well aware of the wonderful feeling when the rational brain fades away, and the emotional eating-charged brain turns on. This process trains the brain to want more food. Food is all around us, and porn ads, like weight-loss programme ads, are often waiting on the sidebar and bottom of most news and sports sites.

When the emotional eating/over-exercising cycle is over, the rational brain kicks back in, and the shame cycle does its entrée. The control pilots have been released and returned to the cockpit.

Reality strikes hard. "*I promised myself I would never do that again.*" I can just imagine how it must feel when the porn show is over. Emptiness. Guilt. Shame. Loneliness. Isolation.

Once the feelings of worthlessness and hopelessness build, it becomes overwhelming. You look for something to make these feelings go away. Something that will override the shame. And the process starts all over again.

In today's society, we are surrounded by people seeking gratification in all kinds of guises. Consider the last time you craved a bar of chocolate, or sought to reward yourself with a cake, for a job well done, or a bottle of wine after a hard week at work. Now consider that same desire getting out of control. Something went wrong, and you reached for one biscuit and then another, soon the whole packet had disappeared. Later feeling guilty, you need something else, bigger and better, so you order a takeaway and crack open the wine. All the while, you are anticipating the reward of feeling good. This is dopamine at its finest. Now you may not like this behaviour, but it has become a habit.

The habit is because of something called neuroplasticity. Imagine these to be grooves in your brain that have, over time, become deeper and deeper as you do the same old thing time and time again. Perhaps to explain better, consider a slightly wonky garden gate. Each time you open the gate, it scrapes over the concrete causing a groove to be created. It would be better to realign the gate to stop this from happening. But that's easier said than done because you are busy doing other things.

Let's go back to dopamine. This is about learning that rewards feel good so that we can repeat the process. Usual activities, like having sex, eating cake, riding fast motorbikes, watching sports or masturbating delivers a reward.

Imagine a man who moves from one woman to the next. The hunter tracks down women using his charm, inviting them to participate in some form of sexual gratification. His reward was the anticipation of the chase and the win, not necessarily the sex. What drives him, and people like him, is the newness and the novelty. That's why you hear of serially unfaithful people. They promise that this is the last time, but their neurotransmitters and neuroplasticity are such that they are driven to continue. This behaviour becomes a pattern for these people's lives, and dopamine likes a pattern.

One of the many questions I ask myself is, how does abuse change the brain? One of my patterns is that I am addicted to risk. I can remember wanting to prove to others that I could do things that they were not able to do. I wanted to be admired for doing crazy stuff. Outside of school, I was daring. I almost died once, from jumping off a cliff. I wanted to have shock-value, and look daring and impressive like Robert Smith, of The Cure. I wanted to show off, and I didn't want to be pretty; I wanted to be a super cool rebel. Then, contrary as ever, I wanted to be beautiful.

I was in control and out of control. Some have even said that I was a control freak. A sensitive control freak. I needed control over myself, my body and how I presented myself. I wanted to control what other people thought of me. I wanted everyone to like me.

It is only now, years later, that I realise what a lucky escape I have had. My brain and self-image led me down one path, but somehow I managed to escape completely destroying my life. I was shocked to read the 2003 report '*Food for Thought: Substance Abuse and Eating Disorders*', where the findings said that individuals with eating disorders are up to five times likelier to abuse alcohol or illicit drugs, and those who abuse alcohol or illicit drugs are up to eleven times more likely to have eating disorders.

Like me, the addicts that I am trying to understand are seeking connection and love. It is easy to judge what others do without knowing their reasons, or the life experiences that have led them to this point, isn't it?

It has been the awakening of my passion and vision to end human trafficking for commercial sexual exploitation that has saved me. The more I learn about why these things are happening, the more I learn about myself. Knowing how our brains are wired, we can better understand how consumer patterns fulfil needs and choices. My dream is to be able to achieve this with the same fighting spirit I displayed in my childhood midsummer games, combined with elegance, wisdom and intelligence.

Pause for thought

On December 4th, 2020, Nicholas Kristos from *The Economist* said, "*Pornhub prides itself on being the cheery, winking face of naughty, the website that… …donates to organisations fighting for racial equality and offers steamy content free to get people through Covid-19 shutdowns*" There is more to this story. Kristos's research found that *Pornhub* attracts 3.5 billion visits a month. This results in more clicks than on websites like *Netflix*, *Yahoo* or *Amazon*. Every day, *Pornhub* earns money from almost three billion advertising impressions.

The foremost reason why I do not want my own, or any, children's brains to be hijacked by *PornHub* is their exposure to the videos of child rapes, racist and misogynist content and footage of women being asphyxiated in plastic bags. How could we ever explain to children why anyone would like to either watch this, or want the children to watch anyone being suffocated and raped?

What is shocking to me as a mother, is that if anyone searches (as Kristos says) for *girls under18* (no space) or *14yo*, more than 100,000 suggestions will be offered, of which many are images and videos of children being raped. [v]

Following his report, *Pornhub* found themselves in a sticky situation with payment providers, for example, removing their services. One has to ask why they hadn't done any due diligence in the first place. It still astounds me that they were able to remove around 10 million offending videos, like the ones I describe above. [vi]

I consider myself to be an average moral and ethical human. However, I have discovered that no matter how normal you are, we are, to some extent, at the mercy of our hormones. For most of us, this means that we will naturally struggle with things like overeating or binge drinking at the weekend. Perhaps shovelling down a whole packet of biscuits when the day feels sour.

Pornography addiction is much more involved than stuffing down biscuits or just wanting to look at nude videos and pictures. It has a deep connection to the chemicals in our brain, as you will have read. Your brain on porn is much more complicated than you think.

As one might imagine, it's easier to ask for help for a food addiction than a porn addiction. Likewise, it would probably be easier to admit to your employer that you're an alcoholic, rather than a porn freak, sitting with your hand in your pants during your lonely moments, in front of a non-judgmental computer.

Masturbation to pornographic videos includes the extra stimulating and relaxing atmosphere of total privacy. It offers the forbidden in combination with pleasure. And herein lies a dilemma, because as Dr. Gail Dines, author, TED talk speaker and founder of *Culture Reframed*, puts it:

"We know from 40 years of research that the younger boys get to porn, the more it limits their capacity for intimacy, the more it decreases their empathy for rape victims, the more it increases depression and anxiety, and the more likely they are to engage in risky sexual behaviour... now we have a generation of boys desensitised [to violence against women]." [vii]

What, you may wonder, is the answer to this? How do we, through legislation and regulation, change the nature of the market for pornographic material? I expect all stakeholders to take responsibility. First, everyone who has authority in deciding which websites are publishing stuff based on the exploitation of people, such as *Google*, *Amazon*, the *European Court of Justice*, world governments, legal societies and the *Ministry of Justice*, should, in my opinion, legislate and agree on the banning of pornographic advertising. Next, eliminate all possibility of anonymity through the requirement for electronic registration with a social security number or the like. Then it becomes not only a conscious responsibility and choice to consume pornography, but you can be identified as doing so.

Earlier, I said that the Credit Card companies *VISA* and *Mastercard* have taken a stand and blocked *PornHub* from their payment services. This is to be applauded, along with countries that have prohibited pornographic Internet websites. However, in many hotels, you can watch porn from your hotel room. Not only that, to get around the laws, *PornHub* has now launched its own VPN service *VPNHub*. It is a service that people can use, if *PornHub* or something else is blocked in the country they are in. *PornHub* states that it has around a thousand servers in 15 different countries to redirect their user traffic. So it looks as if the user is surfing from a country where *PornHub* is not blocked. The lengths that this company will go to, to serve depravity are astonishing.

There is never an easy solution to protecting your children from what they will inevitably encounter on social media platforms. And as a parent, you may feel overwhelmed. The best way to deal with this is to talk with your children and encourage an honest debate. We know from the plethora of sites emerging and the lengths that a site like *Pornhub* will go to, that there will always be dangers from porn sneaking in.

To support you, I have included a list of resources to "*The Porn Conversation*" that explain how to inform your children about the many websites that are based on exploiting people against their free choice of life and will. You will learn how human trafficking, filmed rapes, and violent porn are related. And if you do not know how to introduce these discussions, refer to movements like "*Fight The New Drug*" or "*Culture Reframed*". They offer excellent material for parents, teachers and other adults for talks with young people about pornography. "*Porrfri barndom*" is a Swedish organisation working towards a childhood free from porn. Like they so wisely say: "*You cannot replay a childhood*".

Chapter 5

"The cause of women's overrepresentation in modern slavery, is a broader pattern of human rights violations, crimes that disproportionately affect women and girls. These include violence in close relationships and sexual violence, discriminator perceptions of women's ownership, as well as access to education and citizenship". The Walk Free Foundation Global Slavery index Report 2018

The inner journey

Life is both a journey and an adventure. It has taken me to where I have needed to go, despite thinking I was going to where I wanted to be. I have learned that we are all being guided by an invisible thread that weaves the rich tapestry of our lives. Nothing is by accident. It is all by design. I have come to understand that there is a richness of patterns of behaviour, challenges, lessons, and incredible gifts in every story. This experience has been so many things - an emotional, physical and spiritual exploration. Every part of everything is meshed together and has helped me to become who I am.

My love of travelling has taught me so much about not only myself but others' lives, how they live and especially their challenges. Some of these things have been shocking and have certainly woken me up. I do not know if this has made me a better human, but it has given me a reason for being my own personal best. In all of these interactions, I know that the nature of my brain shifts, my neural pathways change, and my memories gather to remind me of where I have been, but who I am becoming is yet to be discovered.

Some of my most beautiful memories and experiences have been my awakenings to women's magic. I didn't need to travel one mile physically but, within, I went to the furthest reaches of the Universe and back. Women are fascinating. You may be one yourself and take for granted how amazing you are. I want to ask you, how do you feel in the company of other women? For most of my life, I have felt uncomfortable and insecure in women's groups. What has scared me to death is the strength and sensuality that all women seem to possess, even if they do not let it show, or even know that they hold such power. Although there are strong bonds between myself and my girlfriends, I confess it took me half a lifetime to understand the need for girls' parties, ladies' clubs and women's networking groups. Perhaps I have felt overwhelmed or confused at how they gathered in exclusive social circles, where I had never felt a sense of belonging?

In school, I would watch with envy at the clusters of girls who naturally exchanged gossip and laughter. I was never a part of this seemingly closed community. Even when I was invited to parties, I would wonder why and then I became fearful of how one was supposed to behave. They appeared to have a vast knowledge of the world. It seemed you would need a special concession to join in their secret society.

I have a vivid memory of when I had taken a skipping rope to school, or as I call it, a jump rope. Before this time, I would cautiously skirt around the recess where large groups of girls would gather. The groups seemed impenetrable, and I did not know who I could trust. Like all schools, there are the group leaders who rule their fans with an invisible iron hand. Woe betide anyone who broke their hidden rules. They weren't evil, but looking in from the outside, you could see that there was always a terrible power struggle going on. On this day, I wondered who I would share my rope with? I wanted to be friends with everyone and for them all to like and accept me.

What I really wanted, but dared not voice, was that I wanted to be the leader in both of the groups. With my dad as such a strong role model, this made perfect sense. I felt so much more in tune with men while, at the same time, rather curious about the energy of women. There was a scent and a sexual radiance I could sense, which confused me. The females were competitive, but differently from men, and I certainly didn't know how to step in and become their leader.

Patriarchy is a fascinating system to learn about, yet so many are fearful and despise it. We have been taught to hate it because it has come to mean gender inequality and the suppression of the feminine. Men creating and implementing laws that benefit only men have to be anathema to women. It seems such a twisted way for a society to behave. Favouring one sex over the other. I see it from many angles.

On the one hand, there are the social rules created by men that appear to hold women down and, on the other hand, a system of structures that are very logical in their approach. I wonder what would society be like if it had been designed by women. Would the men be where we are, fighting for their rights and complaining that the matriarchy was powerful and abusive? It's a debate that I believe will rage on forever and not one I care to bring too much more energy to. Experience tells us that there has been great inequality and oppression throughout all of society. I believe that it has proven to be a part of the problem rather than the solution in my work. In my family, though, the patriarchy describes our family dynamics.

Women, I believe, can learn a lot about men, such as how to use their warm Yang energy to, for example, set goals and achieve them. Of course, all humans possess both Yin (female) and Yang (male) energy. However, as we grow up, I have witnessed that we naturally move towards one way of being. Most of us end up out of balance - just like society.

My experiences have shown me that society has tended to reward the attributes of male energy more than the female. Setting goals and striving to do more suppresses our more open, receptive, allowing, nourishing and intuitive qualities. Let's face it, how do you measure intuition? What are clever, smart goals and plans, as opposed to intuitive knowing? Regardless of this pondering, I have ended up very much like my family before me, working alone or only with close family, because of how I was brought up.

I chose this way of living and working, because the imbalance I came to witness time and time again, between the feminine and the masculine in the corporate world, made it impossible for me to work there and maintain good health. In this environment, I received a massive wake up call that left deep tracks in my soul.

In 2007, as we were planning our return to Sweden, following a year of volunteering in Asia after the tsunami disaster, I was asked if I wanted to join and create an outreach project between NGOs and companies in developing countries. Can you imagine my delight? I was so happy! They had asked me! I felt so important, valued and valuable. I looked forward to finally being able to make a difference at a higher level.

We were so caught up in a whirl of making plans and creating connections with key people, that I missed the spin that pushed us into becoming a Corporate Social Responsibility consulting company instead. I became the CEO. It must have been because I radiate so much masculine energy and power that they thought I would be a perfect leader. I wanted to lead, and here I was, a square peg in a round hole. Those who knew me could see that this was wrong. By nature, I am an inspirational leader, not a dictator. If only I had said no, I could have saved my family and myself from the monster I became. Despite being brought up in a male-dominated environment, I felt more and more stifled by the overpowering male energy and started to burn out. It seems strange, looking back, that I had lived all my life surrounded by masculine energy, yet here the suppression of my Yin and femininity crushed me. I did what many do, and I played a role that I thought was expected of me. Can you relate to any of this?

Visualise the scene. I am sure you will have experienced it too, every morning pasting on a mask and hiding the salty tears that flowed into my heart. Smiling all the time for my family, who watched me be the first to leave and the last to come home. Soon I didn't want to go and started to experience panic attacks. Who on Earth was I, crumbling on the inside while delivering authoritative advice on sustainability? Looking back with some scepticism, I think I made the perfect leader for this group of people, as I was easy to influence and steer in the direction they wanted. They appeared so talented with their impressive knowledge of sustainability issues as they pursued their ambitious desires. I was too weak to protect myself adequately and constructively. I felt small in their company, and this only served to exacerbate my shame. I was so locked into this that I was unaware of how they were gently trying to get me out of the company. In retrospect, I was foolhardy to have stayed so long. A different playground yet still confusing.

Thankfully, I was flung off that hamster wheel and into another adventure – Yoga. It was during my first Yoga teacher training (silly term, actually, since we are all practitioners of a lifelong education), that I began to realise the magnitude of the feminine, and what power banks women's groups are. Can you envisage what it felt like stepping into that cold hall for the first time? I was both envious and insecure. One moment I was in the middle of twenty-two seemingly confident women. As I glanced around, I could sense my vulnerability rising and my courage leaving. The next moment, I experienced beautiful gratitude for just being alive. In the third moment, I felt sad about not being generous enough in my life.

The Yoga anatomy classes were boring. However, I loved sitting in a circle with these women, listening to acknowledgements, confessions, life misery and life crises. Existential ponderings were mixed with questions about life's everyday puzzles. Yoga Sutras, stories told by Yoga masters of long ago, were brought alive, analysed and interpreted by my fellow sisters. It was a revelation. I found myself asking if I really did have permission to sit in this beautiful female energy for a whole weekend? Was this allowed? Was I allowed to really lift the lid off the hidden and the forgotten? I wasn't sure. After all, would it mean that I would be betraying the clan if I let slip any of their secrets, and so I was careful not to?

On the Yoga mat, emotions would come to the surface without warning. Yoga acts as a guide to help you find inner peace through love and compassion for yourself and others. The learning is sometimes beautiful and often challenging. You can choose to meet these lessons with acceptance or resistance. The former is most difficult but preferable in the long run since the resistance strikes back when you least expect it. So, through Yoga, I have started to learn acceptance, to give in, let go, and to surrender, but also to not give up. However, the most important thing I learned is that women's groups are assets and not threats.

The practice of Yoga puts the light on the inner journey. It provides the power and responsibility to change our way of living. I couldn't have pictured so much transformation at the moment I heard, "who in here could not imagine teaching Yoga?" The question echoed in the room, and I froze. I had only been thinking about engaging in Yoga postures, the chakra system, and understanding more of the philosophy of Yoga. There was no thought other than being a student. Now an opportunity was opening up, and it would be possible for me to guide others. Inside I quaked, now I would have to reveal a part of my inner self and become entwined with others' projections and feelings. I had a choice. To let the adventure slip through my sweaty palms or to dare to jump. I still didn't believe that I could do this. Two of us put our hands up. I turned to look at the face that belonged to the other hand. I was caught by her dark beauty and sparkling blue eyes. How could someone like her be as afraid as me?

The resistance would not go. I felt so angry, so outside of the group, so lonely and invisible. Why was I even here? In this room, women with dreams, wisdom, confidence, strength and beauty rocked my head with questions. I could feel that trembling inner child of mine cry that this was not fair. Why do I feel so ugly? Where is my beauty? How do I get what they have? Every insecurity I had suppressed seemed to want to leap from Pandora's Box.

Worse was to come — sessions where we had to share words about what we saw in others. As the words "transparent", "honesty", and "exciting" came out, my petulance rose. I wanted "female", "charismatic", and "sexy". All of this whirled around me as my yearnings and longings rose up and felt like a ton of bricks to crush me even further. Gradually, it dawned on me that I would always be yearning for something until I learned to love and appreciate myself. These women, and the women before them, have enabled me to wake up and have given me unexpected lessons and beautiful gifts. They have taught me how to trust other women. I had to learn how to meet their femininity, see their strength, and dare to believe that I, too, possessed the power, beauty, and confidence they radiated. What we see in others, we have to have inside of us, don't we?

Things started to fall into place, and I could feel my self-esteem improving. Where once it was about self-confidence through performance and results - instead of how good you are, and how we won over the opposition, or how we succeeded in our investments so that the results surpassed the budget - this year again! Instead, self-esteem began to take its place, allowing me to accept and forgive myself and others - with an open heart. Good self-esteem does not depend on the affirmation of others. A person with good self-esteem has confidence, knowledge of who she is and has the capacity to listen with an honest and open attitude.

Self-confidence is temporary. Once confirmed through performance, it can quickly turn into a craving. Self-esteem, contrarily, is enduring since it includes accepting oneself, encompassing all our good qualities and personalities, along with all our faults and flaws. An honest and non-judgmental approach is based on healthy self-esteem from the ground up. This is what I strive for on my inner journey.

Learning about balancing male and female energies in the Yogic tradition enabled me to make more sense of how to find inner peace. I discovered the philosophy behind our energy centres, called the Chakras. These are located in a line along our spine, beginning with the Root Chakra in the pelvic floor, and ending with the Crown Chakra, at the top of the head. All Chakras contain both feminine and masculine energies. When balance exists between the feminine and masculine energies, you feel harmony, flow and contentment. These opposites live within us. Sun and moon. Light and dark. Day and night. Inhalation and exhalation. Inspiration and exploration. One does not exist without the other. Everything in life is about balance — balanced eating, balancing the books, balanced views and balanced energies. Tuning into ourselves and balancing is an essential part of being able to manifest what we want in the world. This is the spectrum we travel all day long. Mostly unaware of what is happening. Just as we are unaware that at all times, our body is balancing its systems, right down to the cells, in every moment.

Here on the mat in the stillness of my being, I listened, and I soon realised why my wagon had tipped over so many times. I had been driven by greed, envy, stress and overdoing. Without thinking about it, I had been behaving and feeling according to the cultural expectations and notions of how we "should" relate to these as man and woman. Soon I was to become hooked on Yoga. Through Asanas, the physical postures, I was able to achieve a better-balanced system. By understanding where the underlying energetic imbalances lay, I could now change how I was in the world - a lovely person to hang out with.

Of course, I have not been an overnight success; I have a long way to go for total balance, but I am happy when I succeed momentarily. What I have come to know is that, through our actions, we show our masculine power, while the feminine energy shows who we are. Masculinity stands for doing, and femininity stands for being and becoming. It is not a question of good or bad. It is an implicit fact that duality exists. We cannot make progress by merely doing or just being. Both are needed. I often wonder what others do to balance their energy when there is so much going on in this multifaceted world. Do they even notice if they are or not? Are they aware of the masculine and feminine of their own constitution?

For me, it is imperative to honour both the masculine and feminine and to embrace them in my inner journey to becoming my best self. It is so much nicer to hang with someone who is able to balance feminine and masculine energy. With a united internal force, I can stay focused and on track. For all of us, the balancing of these energies has real-world consequences. Imagine a world where there is more harmony and freedom from those oppressive forces that create and demand human exploitation. Imagine an army of loving humans who know who they are and accept it. Then we would be more creative, loving and kind. When we are in balance, we can stay focused and be flexible when the wind changes. Grounded people are able to see clearly their vision, and to communicate their strong will. Let us, therefore, be balanced and grounded and send our "feel-good-energy" whenever possible. Isn't it always possible?

Life goes in revolutions (fast stuff) and evolutions (slow stuff). Neither exists without the other, and both exist because of the other. Revolution originally comes from the way in which the planets revolve. When I think about revolution, what comes to mind are fights, wars, battles, disorder, governments being overthrown, blurred lines, no winners and certainly nothing remotely predictable. But I also feel that revolutions can be born out of a desire to create change quickly. People who subscribe to revolution want to crush old ways and make way for new order but not necessarily with that associated fear, frustration and anger. Revolution can be about resolution without obliteration. Revolution can be about innovation, creativity, and change for the good but with rapid growth pains.

The word and idea of revolution can seem misdirected and misunderstood. On the one hand, it is born of hope and for a new way, by people who want change and to create a new order. Yes, it can get rid of the nasty stuff, create a shift in power and has a place. I am not talking about a revolution that causes death and destroys lives; I am talking about the industrial, technological, entrepreneurial and conscious revolutions which pave the way for people to change the way that they live.

Evolution is a process, which comes from the feminine core that keeps us awake, aware and alive. From a connection and collaboration of mind, body, soul, and spirit – our energy (vibrational signature and conscious connection). It is tied to the gradual changes that have taken place, which have altered how we live.

Think for a moment of every revolution in your life. Times of abrupt change, followed by times of quiet consideration. Eruptions, solitude, eruptions, quietude, and so your world revolves and evolves.

My journey to becoming a more authentic me and trying to be a voice for others has been an incredible and never-ending adventure. It's a process where I am learning how to harness my power and not the conditioning handed down from my family or the world around me. I'd like to think that this cruise, which has taken extraordinary effort and courage, will genuinely enable me to fulfil my purpose.

Pause for thought

Every day, people are being affected by things that are increasing their levels of stress and anxiety. Many more are feeling unexplained emotions, angry, depressed, fearful and dissatisfied with life. What tends to happen is that we blame external sources, instead of looking within and seeking inner peace through going on a journey of self-inquiry and self-discovery. Yoga has been something that has supported my path through life. You can undoubtedly survive without practising Yoga however, with it, life takes on a new meaning.

The main philosophy of Yoga is simple: mind, body, and spirit are all one. The word Yoga means "*union*" or to unite. Yoga has the potential to change your life, but does not offer a simple solution to all of life's challenges. Control freaks are likely to become "*Yoga control freaks*", and those who strive for success are probably also trying to achieve "*Yoga success*". We all have negative patterns that we get lost in.

Yoga gives us a chance to look honestly at our lives and life patterns. This requires both courage and commitment to try something new, but it will probably be worth the effort.

There is significant scientific evidence demonstrating that Yoga postures and *Pranayama* (breathing exercises) can accelerate healing and rehabilitation processes in traditional healthcare. In addition, many doctors testify about how Yoga and meditation can increase physical and mental health, and thus contribute in many ways to society.

The physical poses called *Asanas*, practised together with controlled breathing, cognitively balance your right and left brain. The scientific study of Yoga demonstrates that mental and physical health are closely allied, bringing a sense of harmony and unity. Yoga is empowering, and one of the greatest benefits is that the student becomes their own healer.

The practise of Yoga can mean different things to different people. My experience is that Yoga is much better than many other alternatives. I feel a greater sense of wellbeing, allied with a low risk of injury when I practise. It also contains wonderful techniques to find out who you are, who you want to become and what you have to offer. As the body gets stronger, so does the mind.

One aspect, that I especially identify with, is that within most Yoga communities, there is an alliance with an unspoken but clear agreement to live an ethical lifestyle, supported by spiritual practise. This includes caring for your body as the vehicle that transports you around, working out physically, breathing mindfully to manage effortless meditation, and raising your awareness.

Yoga is a journey (not a destination) in our individual vessels, with ties to everyone else's ship. Imagine if all crafts pulled in the same direction for revolution and evolution to heal humanity. Yoga means union, where uniting the body, mind and spirit results in balance on the Yoga mat, and in everyday life. Living Yoga is about giving back some of the Prana [life energy] through various philanthropic efforts, whether voluntary work after disasters, projects against human trafficking or just a smile for a neighbour. I wouldn't be surprised if bullying in schools or the crime rate in society, in general, went down if we made Yoga and meditation a natural part of our daily routine. Yoga for children builds confidence, compassion, connection, awareness, mindfulness, and gently introduces discipline. Because Yoga encourages your inner light to shine, you can imagine our children becoming amazing global citizens and carrying out this work.

And finally, Yoga asks beautiful questions like *who are you?*, a*re you doing what you really want?, and are you true to yourself?* These are important questions to ask ourselves regularly, so as to stay true to who we are. Whatever the answers to these questions, the following statement keeps coming back: *To make a change, you have to start with yourself.* If you want to improve someone else's life, you have to start with your own. I hope that we can change the world, one Yogi at a time.

So, let's start here and now. Shall we?

Chapter 6

"By working to raise awareness of women's issues and improving their social and economic status, ABC Nepal aims to combat gender discrimination in all its forms, so women are valued for the people we are, rather than the price somebody is prepared to pay for us." Durga Ghimire, founder of ABC Nepal

Awakening

Of all the women I have met, there is one who has aroused my greatest admiration and my greatest wonder. Steady like a rock, she stands when all of us around her are swept away by love, ambition or hubris. She rarely has a strong opinion because she does not judge anyone. She doesn't gossip because she accepts us all as we are. In her eyes, I could see sadness every time we moved abroad and took her grandchildren far away. She did not say a word. She kept her thoughts to herself. However, between the lines, I could hear that she did not understand so many of my choices. In her eyes and heart are the family secrets. Like a rock, she stands steady and supportive — my mother.

Not everyone is given the chance to enjoy a safe childhood. Yet every child deserves one. I was one of the lucky ones whose parents provided me with excellent foundations, so much so that I feel perfectly at home wherever I lay my hat. Strong family foundations don't just happen. It takes intentional choices to create them. In our family, everyone is valued as an individual. We have strong bonds of love. We acknowledge each other's strengths and support each other even when we are not sure what they are up to. However, a paradox arises when I try to identify where I belong. I definitely belong with and to my family. Yet, there is that part of me who wants to wander around the globe because of my insatiable curiosity to settle elsewhere. I can walk into practically any hotel room in the world and know that this is home, albeit a temporary one. I suppose it is because of my strong roots, I also belong to the world, like a global citizen. My desire is to feel at home anywhere and create a safe home for my fellow travellers, i.e. my family.

Home isn't my house. It is more of a feeling of belonging to the world community and doing things that matter, such as justice, equality and freedom. In this global home, I have the privilege to meet and work with incredible people and witness extraordinary healing.

It was stress that caused our first family adventure abroad. The idea of travelling far was ignited by a feeling that something had to change, or we would continue to go around in circles. At the time, our second daughter was newly born, and we ran like squirrels on a wheel, trying to manage two companies, two children and squeeze in some family time in our busy work schedule. One day my husband and I looked at each other and said, "What if.....", "Yes, let's do it." Can you imagine the relief and subsequent excitement? It was like a line had been drawn in the sand, and we could sit a while and draw breath. You already know about our great Australian adventure from Chapter 2.

Coming home was interesting, especially for our children. I will never forget their reaction to the Swedish introverted silence at the bus stops. After a year among Australia's outspoken people, they were used to interaction whenever possible. We still miss the many playful visits to the parks, the BBQs and the easy outdoor living that made life so laid back and free from stress. It is a perfect place for a young family to create strong bonds.

A desire to discover more of the world's diversity had been aroused. Three and a half years, or 1 278 days later, it was finally time for a new expedition. You will undoubtedly remember Boxing Day 2004 when one of the largest tidal waves, a tsunami, struck southern Asia. Around 225,000 people were indiscriminately swallowed by the sea. Mercilessly, the wave swept houses, family members, documents, moms and dads away like a furious giant. It had no discernment and annihilated everything in its path. It was an act of nature, an earthquake under the sea, on which humanity had no influence.

Thousands of Swedes had celebrated Christmas in Thailand, of which 543 never returned home. One of these was a cousin of our children's friend, who lived a few streets away from our Swedish home. We did not know about this before setting out. Later, we understood how the tsunami wave created another disaster within that family, causing a different kind of tidal wave between the parents. The father's view was that as they were able to keep two of their three children, they had been given a gift. The mother only mourned the lost child.

I think most people would feel hatred towards such cruelty. So did I. To witness how a child can be torn out of his mother's arms, I imagine it raises powerlessness and anger. I was angry too, but a tiny part of me felt excitement. The tsunami disaster gave me a reason to travel, a reason to reach out, and a reason to do something that mattered. It allowed me to be part of the healing power in our world. It gave me a chance to be someone that counts. Someone who could make a difference.

Within months of the disaster, we had bought tickets to Thailand, rented our house, put our things in storage, and booked a hotel in Phuket which would be our temporary home during our house-hunting process. We had done this once before, during our maternity gap year in Australia. This time, thankfully, it was a much smoother operation.

Our grand adventure Down Under during 2002 had given us perspectives and experiences of changing environments. Being newcomers, referred to as "the Swedes", strengthened our group affiliation and made us bond as a family in an incredible way. Also, we saw how this year gave our children an outstanding education in global citizen behaviour. Through interaction with children, mostly from Australia and nearby countries, our daughters had to learn English, adapt to new environments and above all, make themselves understood by playing with other children who spoke another language. This is about building bridges between cultures on a deep level. We watched and learned. We saw how poorly the indigenous people, the Aborigines, had been treated and pushed into poverty, which often led to drug abuse and begging. I understood that I had a message to spread, to educate the world about peaceful relations and respect for other cultures. Many years later, my vision would be refined to putting an end to the fact that we are still trading human beings in the 21st century. This has to stop.

This time, 2006, our move was under very different circumstances and one with a mission. As you can imagine moving a family of five abroad is a logistical, administrative and practical sudoku. Unlike sitting peacefully with a logic-based, combinatorial number-placement puzzle, scanning rows and columns, eliminating numbers or squares and finding situations where only a single number can fit into a single square, we had to juggle everyone's needs almost simultaneously. Applications to schools had to be arranged. It was essential that the visa process was done in the right order and our finances meticulously budgeted. Not to mention various team-building skills so that the family relationships remained grounded and stable. Every new experience teaches you more about family and human dynamics.

Naturally, we wanted to team up with someone who knew more about Thailand and the disaster. It's always tricky to know how to be the best help. Since we had three small children at that time, we could not be of much help in the midst of the sick and wounded. Therefore, we started researching how we could use our economic knowledge and business skills to reach out and help to rebuild the infrastructure. We had made contact with a microcredit foundation that had given small loans to business owners and family providers on Phi Phi Island, one of the hardest hit areas because of its flat landscape and exposed location in the Indian Ocean.

I had called Johan Stael von Holstein, a Swedish entrepreneur who had spent a lot of time in Thailand, and who wanted to support the reconstruction of the infrastructure. He literally flew to Thailand with two suitcases filled with money. There is a lot of prestige in the "aid industry", and since Thailand's government did not consider their nation to be a developing country, they did not want to accept Holstein's offer. It all ended with Mr Holstein being persona non grata in the country. However, this man does not take no for an answer. Regardless, he founded the Swedish Microcredit Foundation with money from his own pocket, and a bunch of Swedish Hotel owners in Phuket. They wanted the Foundation to provide microloans to entrepreneurs / islanders / family providers who had had their businesses literally washed away. It became our task to verify the contracts, ensure that the mortgages were paid according to plan, and coach entrepreneurs to rebuild their operations. Our work also included determining who had the greatest need.

During our year there (July 2006 - July 2007), we met many people who had lost everything - even many close family members. With help from small loans, they could slowly build their new lives and support themselves and their families. What made this project work so effectively was the nature of the projects and the source of the funds. The administration costs were low, and the decisions were made instantly. We did not have to wait for paperwork and signatures, in order to solve future problems on the spot. It was wonderful to be a part of a team providing microcredits to around 300 small business owners and heads of families. The businesses were made up of fruit sellers, masseurs, jewellery vendors and tourist guides with the long-tail boats, among other things. Surprisingly given the nature of the disaster and continuing after-effects, 70% of the loans were repaid within two years.

It will come as no surprise to know that this place, full of tragedy and hope, felt like home. I was definitely at home. The tropical weather, the friendliness, sense of spiritual oneness, spicy and nutritious food, the sea, and our family gathered together in paradise, made me feel complete. However, this was not a holiday. Our call to action had a purpose: which was to make a difference to the people, the economy and in the name of the ones who were washed away so cruelly that day.

Thai culture is family first. Families typically live in close proximity, where it is relatively unknown for anyone to live in isolation. My own home, miles from here, had taught me about the heart of family life, but now I needed to learn how to live outside of that. I was carried by the memories of each of them held in my heart, to which I added many new stories from my new family. Along with the treasures from home, I also brought my baggage and unnecessary belongings with me. There were many times when I had to put my prejudices on hold, for example, during the collaboration with the local employees, Tee and Aor.

Aor (pronounced as the letter "o" in "four") was a Muslim family man with 4 children, one wife and one "little wife". Aor and his "little wife" slept in the attic of the office together, while his wife and four children lived in a house he had proudly built by himself. He used to say: "*I am a very good man. I only have one wife and one girlfriend. That man over there, he is bad. He has four wives, and he cannot support even one."*

Tee was a young, very humble Buddhist whose dream was to travel the world and make a career for himself. He always begged me not to forget about him and to help him advance in his work. His transparent view of the world taught me a lot about how the Buddhists and the Muslims lived beside each other on Phi Phi Island without any significant problems or any major contradictions. The more we got to know the different cultures, the more we realised that the root cause of wars can never be religion, but the pure and intense power struggle over assets and people. If the Buddhists on the island did not try to convince the Muslims that their faith was right and vice versa, harmony could exist. The Phi Phi Island's inhabitants' only goal was to survive in the best way possible and take advantage of the great tourism industry. This became very clear after the tsunami, because everyone's goal was to rebuild the hotels, restaurants, diving and snorkelling businesses, massage studios, and fruit stands so that visitors could return to the island as quickly as possible.

Together with Tee and Aor, we used to walk around the island and visit all the families and business owners who owed money to SMF and collect the payments, instalments, and amortisations. Most people paid back, but depending on which culture they came from, they had a hard time understanding the concept of a "loan", and paying back the borrowed money. Slowly, I realised the advantage of having this odd couple as co-workers. Aor understood how a Muslim person looked at a loan. Tee had the noble art of mediation in his blood.

One story that still amuses me was that of the long tail boat owner, whose outboard motor apparently sank over and over again, meaning that he had to ask for more money to continually buy new ones. His problem was that the island was small, and everyone recognised the boats and how they were equipped. When the "sunken" motors suddenly appeared on other boats, we had to convince him that even though I was a woman, I was not stupid and, in fact, I was their boss. The long tail boat owner had to pay back and stop lying.

I shouldn't have been surprised at the way that a small number of people would try to take advantage. Criminality exists everywhere, and especially in paradise. We were often met with a taste of what the other side of this journey was like, as clans not dissimilar to ours closed ranks and used threats to protect what they believed was rightfully theirs.

One night when I was in the small drug store buying something to eat, I got a phone call from Tee. The Tattoo studio owner had spread rumours on the island, with a threat that if we visited him one more time to collect money, an accident might befall us. This is another lesson I learned in Thailand, cowards threaten other people as a projection of their own fear. Only this time, I was terrified. When I went to bed alone after the threat in a bungalow with thin walls, far away from the tourist bars and the crowded main street, I was left with only my fertile imagination. It didn't matter that only one murder had happened during the whole year, despite all the weapons on the island. I prayed that I would not make up a further one. Despite all of this and amid garbage and fallen trees, still not cared for or picked up after the big wave, we felt freedom, purpose and harmony.

We were surrounded by buildings under construction and struggling families who had lost their belongings and sources of income. The wave was never able to wash away their pride. Like the islanders, I, too, felt a deep sense of pride.

Curiosity and adventure had taken us away from one family to another, and now my hat was firmly planted here. What I thought was my purpose being fulfilled was filling my days. What I didn't know was that this would change, and I was soon to discover that the primary goal for the rest of my life would be to work against human trafficking.

Whys arrive at the oddest of times and in the strangest moments. My moment was when I was invited to a home for women with AIDS, the Life Home Project Foundation. We had the privilege of interviewing some of the women. The stories were the same, repeated by different women, about poverty, abuse and mental illness. Stories about men who took advantage of vulnerable women and children because of poverty, were followed by stories about orphans who were trafficked to brothels after the tsunami.

When looking into the women's eyes, I recognised something familiar. Shame. Guilt. It was mainly one woman, whose eyes etched her in my memory. Her skin revealed stress and malnutrition. The lifelessness of her hair shone through, despite her visible attempts to hide it with chemical hair colour. What I mirrored in her eyes was my own shame and guilt. Shame over not being smart enough, successful enough or thin enough. I was thrown back to one time when I was eight years old, and someone counted the rolls of fat on my stomach and compared them to my mum's totally flat belly. A clumsy attempt to make me aware that I was getting a little overweight was, for me, equal to being publicly devalued and judged. The message was clear. You are not good enough as you are. My thoughts went back to the present time and the woman in front of me. It is not hard to imagine her being consistently judged negatively by men who only see a couple of breasts and a vagina. What about her brain - was she ever allowed to share her thoughts or ideas?

Now I felt guilty about not having enough appreciation for my own life. Is this a similar type of shame and guilt the sex buyers feel, when they look at themselves in the mirror after the ejaculation is over?

After our visit, my life purpose was more apparent than it had ever been. I had an awakening. To create as much awareness about human trafficking for commercial sexual exploitation as possible, and to always work against this cruelty. The only thing that I didn't yet know was how? Always the big question, with which I struggle.

There I was in paradise, guided by an invisible thread to this great awakening, knowing and realisation. The trouble was I wasn't sure what the next step would or should be. I knew that I had to stop, let go and surrender. Not an easy task when you are filled with passion and purpose. I had to shake off all the preconceived ideas I had in my head and think. I had found a home for my heart.

Chapter 7

"Modern slavery generates 150 billion dollars within the private sector, of with 99 billion dollars comes from sexual exploitation and the remaining 51 billion dollars from forced labour." Debt slavery means that the worker is indebted to the employer. The worker's services are pawned for repayment of the debt. Worldwide, almost 20% of all trafficking victims are children. UNODC

Longing

Loneliness. Another hotel room. Another journey. Another trip on my own when I escape from my family to get some work done. What was planned to be two days of efficient, hard work ended up with me dwelling on things I didn't need to, crying and doubting myself: I am tired of feeling alone. I have the privilege of being the mother of four children. Sometimes, I wonder how on earth these beautiful souls ended up with me? I am married to an extremely allowing man who actually still wants to hang around with me after 30 years together. I am surrounded by so many networks through schools, neighbours, friends, and yoga communities. Still, I long for something more, something bigger, a more well-organised life or a harmonious existence and, definitely, inner peace. In my eagerness to gain control of life, I continually sign up for new group memberships, training courses and interactive programmes, like "unclutter your home in thirty days", and then discover that they are not for me. The extroverted part of me loves parties, where I am in the spotlight, admired and adored. This part of me longs for the stage and the audience's applause. Alone, in my hotel room, the cold hole within me grows bigger with a deeper hunger for love.

This hole is also a source of wisdom. When I dare to climb in, I know I will find it contains clear answers. And when I do, I find my vision and plan, and I am ready; the extrovert has been fired up, and she is ready to move on to the work. She is ready to network and be seen. This is when she can hand out tasks, delegate responsibilities and make sure everyone is in the right position. But then I am also reminded that I have to pay, if I need my team to take action. There is a fear in the pit of my stomach around paying. I know I need to see it as an investment, but it scares me. I want to be in the quiet, dark hole where it is safe. Herein lies a paradox. The fear of losing it all competes with the excitement of doing business. If only there was a guarantee that the money earned won't just disappear. Who would I be without my wealth? This is when my thoughts tumble into chaos. Is it my intention to build value, or my fear of losing it all that drives me? I know that I will probably never stop calculating the financial risks involved, because this fills me with a sense of security. It makes sense to me that everything is kept in a substantial real estate investment. This gives me the security I crave and the freedom of sometimes being able to leap before I look.

Of course, I do everything knowing I have a solid foundation with minimal risk. Safe. Like my father wanted us to be. Economically safe. That is what he gave us all during his lifetime. He wanted to educate my brother and me on how to build value and wealth. We were too young and immature to understand what a gift he gave to us. Sometimes in the void, I see him, and I hope that even though he has left this world, he feels my gratitude.

Minutes before he died, I leaned into his face; he had to collect all his strength to hear. The Alzheimer's had to step back for a second so that I could whisper, "*We reached The Goal, Dad*".

My dad was a physically strong man with a vulnerable heart who showed me how to overcome addiction with passion. From being a heavy smoker of forty cigarettes per day, overnight, he went to zero. Null. Not a single cigarette touched his lips from that day forward. One morning after a late party with too many flares, accompanied by quite a few whiskeys on the rocks, he came to the conclusion that enough was enough. The fact that my brother and I constantly complained about his bad breath might have helped him decide to extinguish the cigarettes from his life for good. However, knowing my dad, I am sure that watching all the money going up in smoke was his biggest reason. A more compelling addiction for my dad was making money and building value. His obsessively passionate relationship with business and money was a balancing act between risk aversion and hunger for adrenaline.

I long for one more conversation, one more piece of advice from this man who is an integral part of what makes me, me. He has shown me so much dignity not only in life but in his passing. He taught me about value, not only in wealth but what to value and to value who I am. However, I still have those darker moments when I cannot see how I add value to the world.

It's at times like these that I want to crawl back into my hole again, the empty space I call the void (Chapter 12), where dreams can flourish, and I can see everything clearly. Where the howl in my brain is silenced. It's where I can be with me, heal my wounds and just be me. Maybe even find me. The little person who still perceives that the world does care whether she is happy or not. The child who has a sister somewhere in the world who has grown up in another family. It takes deep sorrow to feel euphoric joy in the roller coaster that is life. I feel myself bounce down to the bottom to fester. Then I am pushed up by invisible hands to the sky, where so many possibilities exist. In the emptiness, I meet my life's sorrows and my happiness. I am stuck with the sadness that we are born alone and die alone. Though oddly, in solitude, I find myself and my truths.

Sometimes, though, I am afraid of what I might find in this empty space. Yet, I must go down there to the source, the most immense virtual reality destination ever. In this space, the void, a place where we are all able to travel with our imaginations, be our favourite character, and experience the impossible, which can in real life be transformed into something possible, like my project against human trafficking.

Without my guide and, paradoxically, without distractions, it is so easy to form a business plan. In the creative emptiness that comes from my hysterical chaos, I shape my ideas and find my inspiration. I imagine the stage and see myself performing wonders, while enjoying deafening cheers and applause. Then I remember - you can only get applause if you do something noticeably outstanding. Then I am back to square one. Or at least it feels that way.

Another time that Inspiration comes to me is when a new day starts. I look forward to dawn because when a new day begins, it is an unwritten page. New opportunities in an unspoiled morning. This means I can start over and do better, get fitter, be nicer and become a better person. I long to wake up to a morning when everything falls into place. When I don't have to feel ashamed for not doing enough. For not being enough. A morning that develops into a day when I realise that I am living my dream and our group works as a community towards the same goal. The other side of this hopeful coin is that I long for twilight/dusk so that I can hide what I am not happy with. What I'm ashamed of. The fat on my body. My mistakes and shortcomings. My failures. My melancholy. I sometimes wonder why a day starts so well-intentioned and ends with these dark emotions. Of course, I know that this is all part of what makes me, me and the things I am healing.

When I see the sunrise and lose myself in the sun's kiss, I feel that longing for a life closer to nature, where an endless ocean meets untouched land — an uncluttered world where I can think. I long to find out what I can do. I am transported back in time to the magical land of being a child when everything had so much clarity, and things were so easy and obvious. As an older person, my goals seem more complicated, as I dream of creating a new paradigm. When I hold the golden orb of the sun's potential in my hands, I can feel the energy it gives to my dream. I dream that my social initiative against human trafficking for commercial, sexual purposes leads to reduced demand. Only then will I feel that I have achieved something of value.

Every day when I wake up, I want to challenge myself. I want to provoke. I want to change. I want to stop the cruelty. I want to choose joy. I want to live fully. I long to travel from country to country, from stage to stage, to get my message out. I long to stop the demand for trafficking, particularly in children, for commercial, sexual exploitation.

I long to do a world tour with my dream team that supports my vision of a world where children can just be children and get what children need, in order to grow up to be responsible and happy adults. In this utopia, I can teach them about human rights, but also about human responsibility. Here I can show them a path that leads away from poverty, crime and illiteracy. I know that if we give them the right conditions to thrive, we don't even have to show them the way, because children have inherent knowledge of what they need. It is my belief that the most essential prerequisite for a life filled with opportunities is education.

I long to be part of the positive world development that Hans Rosling and his family write about in their books. He says about his book, Truthfulness, "*This book is my last battle in my life-long mission to fight devastating ignorance... Previously, I armed myself with huge data sets, eye-opening software, an energetic learning style and a Swedish bayonet for sword-swallowing. It wasn't enough. But I hope this book will be." – Hans Rosling, February 2017*. What we learn from him is that today fewer children live in poverty than just 20 years ago. It turns out that many more children nowadays have access to education than when I was growing up. I long to contribute to successes like these. I want to be someone to count on. This is what my heart longs for.

Imagine if all my longings could lead to good things for others. This is what makes my heart sing. My aspirations can and will benefit someone somewhere in our world. I'll be like a domino, sharing my inspiration with someone else's heart, and together we will create a sustainable human cycle for *Feel Good, Do Good*.

My dad started this. I inherited his desire to roll up his sleeves, clean up the mess in the world and start creating some value. As a child, I became aware of our family stories. I could feel the energy in his passion and sense that our stories were containers for change. I sensed that some of our stories would be better not shared with the world. There are always tales that families hide or gloss over and the well-worn ones that seem to get more embellished every time they are told. It is the hidden ones I wonder about. They are the ones that intrigue me.

As a child, I glimpsed the family's well-hidden truths from behind grubby curtains. Peaking into their lives was fascinating. Some of the stories did not make sense. They seemed quite illogical when contrasted with the physical features of the narrators. It was these inconsistencies that revealed the secrets.

On the beach, I spotted a scar above a left groin which piqued my curiosity. It was explained away as a ruptured appendix. In fact, the damage was caused by a gunshot wound that occurred during a police chase in the United States. The penalty for the crime committed was the death penalty by hanging yet, despite this as in all crimes of passion, it just happened. I uncovered that it was a history of infidelity that had aroused such hot feelings.

The appendix story never made any sense. It wasn't until I started to learn about the human body that something stirred in me that someone had been lying. What, I wondered, could the truth be? Imagine watching a gangster movie. Man seduces married woman. The husband finds out and, in a fit of rage, chases the rapscallion responsible. A fight ensues...

This story was hidden in the annals of the family history for years. It is a tale so unbelievable that I thought it should be in a storybook or used as a scene in a gangster movie. It transpires that the key to-this particular storybook was that many a vindictive letter had been posted to the rapscallion's wife, to inform her of her husband's infidelity. Imagine if you had been on the receiving end of something like this, and yet chose to hide the secret so that you could preserve the sanctity of the family?

When I think of this and other stories, I long for a world where there are no more secrets, no matter how incredible they are. I want there to be truth, and to live in a world where truth is a golden and sacred value held by all. Sometimes I wonder if living a life in truth means that other things will need to be sacrificed? What if what you sacrifice provides a steady, stable life at the cost of not following your passion? That doesn't seem tenable for me. I long to hear only my heart and to follow the path that leads me to feel that I have achieved what I came here to do.

Another truth is that we do not see the world as it is. We see the world as we are. If this is the case, then what is my truth or the truth of the family or the industry that I seek to work within? Does knowing the truth about what my heart longs for set me free, and is seeking the truth for a changed world a worthy goal? Is that something of value? Perhaps something that others would value?

My family's truth is that my dad made all of the investments and worked long hours for his family, with pride and honesty in his heart. Where other men may have skipped off to nightclubs and striptease to show off their achievements, my dad brought his colleagues and clients home, where he could show off his family. My heart swells with admiration for this man who would rather drive drunk businessmen home in his own car, than see them making fools of themselves in the city. More than once, valuable key customers have fallen asleep beside us in the back seat of the car, or in the ridge of our boat.

We were taught strong family values, even if other truths were obscured. Like many families, there are children born out of wedlock, and those who will never know their real father. We have an unwritten law that divorce is not an option, let alone having children before marriage. These are our family values. Yet here is my family, ensuring that we are spared from discovering infidelity through a payment slip, designed not to pay an employee, but to pay maintenance for a child recently and discreetly born to a female family member.

It's ironic, really, me calling for change in a vulgar, corrupt industry that pulls a veil over what lies at its heart, whilst my family does the same. Of course, you can't compare the vileness of the porn industry to a family's infidelity. The porn industry paints a different kind of picture, tells a grander story, and then pours innocent lives into the horrific tales they weave. If you look deeper and deeper into the eyes of those caught in the edgy tales, I wonder what longing you will see in their eyes. Do they long to escape and go home, no matter what home is like? Do they long for the latest, hot, sweaty body to finish grinding into them and get it over with, so that they can wash the stinking semen away? Perhaps they long for a sunset like me, because they need the hope for a new and better day.

The lies of generations have to stop somewhere. In my version of the truth, you inherit your ancestors' behaviours until you decide to change and do things differently. This is a time of great awakening and healing. Across the world, people are waking up to the truth of what they carry in their DNA. They long to heal the past and to be the creators of new stories. They long, as I do, to be the inspiration for change.

I long to change the world, as I know so many others would love to do. The question is, how to do it? How would my father do it? This is when I want him back, to ask him what he thinks would be the greatest catalyst for change. I want just one more minute with him, so I can hear his voice say, "*Ulrika, this is what you need to do*". In a way, I guess he hasn't gone away, not really, because I have him in me. He did what he could in the way that he felt would make the most significant impact, and he invested himself in me. Therefore I am changing the world in the way that I view the truths that are contained in my heart, and his. Like me with my dad, it is my wish that minutes before I die, my children whisper in my ear, "*We reached the goal, Mom. We managed that paradigm shift and stopped the demand for human trafficking.*" Can you imagine?

Bronnie Ware, in her book *The Regrets Of The Dying*, talks about what people would have done differently. One of these is what I wish that I'd dared to do, and that is to live a life being true to myself, not the life others expected of me. I'll never really know what others genuinely expected of me, other than to be the best that I can be, to be a light for truth and to follow my heart. I know that my truth and longing have brought me face to face with one of the biggest and most powerful institutions in the world, that ruthlessly focuses on profit, with a selfish interest in the exploitation of innocent people as their pawns. And that feels so big, that sometimes I can't quite believe that my life path brought me here.

When the challenges become overwhelming, I turn to meditation, whereafter my mind becomes a sea of tranquillity. This is when ideas fall effortlessly into my cupped hands. I realise that it is not that I do not have great ideas with which to save humanity. It is knowing which ones will have the greatest impact on the lives I most care about.

As I come back from the Theta rhythm's safe haven and leave behind that space of certainty, I consider that I might lose some of the ground I have just gained, or not benefit from this moment of growth. Yet, I know that it is because I have dared to step into the unknown, and that this is who I have become in the process of turning longing into action, so that I can eventually make a difference.

As I remember my family, their stories, their hidden truths and their desire to change the world for us, I know for sure it is because of their love that I can move forward. I can forget about running away from the things that play out in my head and focus on the lives that matter most to me.

My longing is to break down the walls of dishonesty, shame and guilt, and build new ones out of desire. I look at young girls who long for perfect bodies or celebrity status, which has some of them undergoing plastic surgery and lip enlargement treatments, just to please a commercial ideal. Where do these strange ideas come from? There is a Colombian TV series called *Sin senos si hay paraíso*. The early episodes show powerful drug barons lusting after young schoolgirls, who are groomed, trained, and some lured into a life of prostitution, after they have had colossal breast augmentation. Because small, lithe bodies and big breasts sell. This, according to this programme, is what powerful, rich men want. Is this a truth or a false image fabricated for certain men who might be swayed by these sick ideals? What do the men who purport to have a strong moral compass, and who see women as equal, say about this? What are they doing to prevent being drawn into the stream of opinions that say "*men are bad*"?

You can imagine how easy it is for young women to be drawn into this. I am reminded, when I think of programmes like this, of a time in Cannes in 1986. I was given a business card on the dance floor, with an invitation shouted over the loud music, "*Come to my room at the Ritz Carlton Hotel for a photo session. You have beautiful eyes.*" A dear Italian friend, who was later to become my soul mate, advised me not to go there. So I didn't. What if I had? Where would that have led? That is all it takes, a little tease and flattery, and I could have taken the short walk into the world of grooming, and been recruited into the trafficking industry. It might sound far-fetched, but it is that simple to lure someone away — especially someone who feels alone and confused. Just look at the furore that has been caused by the Epstein case and the grooming done by his girlfriend. They managed it with such ease, luring young girls with temptations for a better life.

One assumes that they appeared like guardian angels to these girls, offering them safety and security from goodness knows what in their lives.

It's strange to think that we all have guardian angels and are being guided, if only we opened our hearts to hear the truth. Despite being surrounded by guardian angels, things can still go wrong, especially if you do not know that they are there. I feel guided by the invisible threads of my family and my heart, and I long to pass this thread out into the world where girls do not have to worry so much, neither about their looks nor allowing themselves to be lured into sex against their will.

Chapter 8

"One child, one teacher, one book, one pen can change the world."[viii] Malala Yousafzai

Educating children

We decided early on that we would take our children to exotic places because we wanted to enrich their zest for life and provide them with a palette of options for the future. They know what it feels like to wake up in the jungle, and have a physical education lesson in the tropical heat. They also know what it feels like to be a stranger, a foreigner, and different. They understand what it feels like to be a visitor in someone else's everyday life. They have classmates and friends from all over the world.

They have learned that breakfast can mean scrambled eggs and dumplings, but also croissants or fried beans. They do not judge anyone by skin colour, religion or accent. They never comment on whether someone has difficulty with the Swedish language, or has different clothes, but often react to how some people interact with others. I am proud of my children and delighted at the way that they have embraced all that life has to offer them. Of course, I am bragging about them, and you may think that I am telling you that they are flawless angels, just as many other mothers would do. However, I am not going to stop. Each day my heart grows with love and admiration for the way that they are growing, and for the contribution that they already make to the world. If parents cannot be rightly proud of their children, then who will? There is plenty of time for them to explore and do things that might attract criticism and obstacles they will have to overcome.

I have this unfailing faith that they are, and will be, amazing just as they are, and this is what they need to hear. Except, of course, when they make poor choices, but these are stories for another day. Right now, what is important is that we teach them that it is ok to be sad or angry, but not to do bad things because you happen to feel this way. My view is that emotionally intelligent children become emotionally intelligent adults. Part of my role as a mum is to be a role model and lead the way in accepting my children's emotions, but not all of their behaviours.

Our children can now adapt easily to new environments and conditions. Like me, they can lay their hats anywhere and be at one with their environment. However, they have no apparent roots in the suburb of Stockholm, where we live. Are they rootless? Perhaps. I hope with all my heart, they see themselves as global citizens, as well as Swedes. I also hope they understand that everything is possible, and that the world is at their feet. Above all, I wish that whatever path they choose, they will do so through free choice.

Naturally, my children did not make the choice to move somewhere new every four years. They were my choices (mine and Stefan's). Sometimes I feel such a contradiction when I think about following my heart and doing it, because I wanted to convince myself that it would be good and beneficial for my children. There is a fusion of motives. On the one hand, there is my belief that part of the intention is altruistic and empathic.

And on the other hand, it is also about pure egoism. In my heart, my hope is that their experiences have given them a more rounded view of the world, and that this will help them to make better choices as they follow their dreams. Although I wanted to teach our children about the world, deep inside a part of me knew that my own inner journey would continue during our expeditions.

Reflecting back, I hope our sojourns and adventures abroad enabled us all to open our minds. It's one thing to say, let's go and be curious, but really is that how you cultivate an open mind? Or is it a part of your personality, or as a result of education and experiences? I think all three. I sometimes wonder what has taught me the most - academic studies or "*the school of life*"?

Not all children get the chance to have a broad education. For them, there are no adventures, let alone any schools or even books to read at home. I adore books. They are where I first lost myself. Do you remember your favourite book from when you were a child? Maybe you cuddled up in the cosy corner of a couch while someone read you the story? Perhaps your parents sat at your bedside, reading you every word of a book you already knew off by heart. And after they kissed you goodnight, you knew that you could fall into a deep satisfying sleep, taking your story with you into your dreams. What if your life was different to this? What if you did not have a book or, if you did, no one took the time to read it to you? This is often the case for children in poor countries, where education is considered a luxury. Because, even if the public schools theoretically are open for every child in most countries, their living conditions make it impossible for them to come to school regularly. Some parents might argue that your time would be better spent on the farm, if it took you four hours to walk to school. They may see these as wasted hours when you have siblings that need looking after and household chores to do. For the majority of families around the globe, school uniforms, books, pens and other school supplies are expensive. The choice might be to buy seed for this year's sowing rather than new shoes for growing feet. In many poor areas, girls are hindered from going to school when they menstruate because there are no sanitary products. Hence, 25% of the time, they cannot go to school.

I am not a big fan of statistics because the data can be modified and adapted to whatever it is you want to convince the reader about. However, I cannot help but pass on these shocking figures regarding the current situation in the inequitable education of the world's children.

- 75 million children miss out on education because of conflict, natural disasters, or other crises.
- A shocking 130 million girls worldwide are not in school.
- In some countries, children are leaving school, still unable to read or write.

Why are 130 million girls worldwide not in school? I found many reasons why on the website, *Malala Fund*. Malala is someone else who knows that there is a bigger purpose for her life. Because of her story and her fearless attitude, she is changing lives. She also has a father who believes in her and her mission. I learned from her site that, in areas where there are few restrictions on child labour, families often choose to let their daughters work instead of studying. Other reasons include child marriages, and typically, as soon as this happens, her education will stop. If girls' education were to continue, there would be a considerable drop in child marriage and adolescent pregnancy.

It will come as no surprise that many of the countries featured have witnessed war and horrific violence which, as a natural consequence, reduces opportunities. Imagine a country having to make a decision to defend all citizens or send its girls to school. This is why, in most countries, the military budget often exceeds the education budget. Without a budget and with so much danger, it's easy to see why most girls do not finish high school. Even if school were an option, many families are so poor they cannot finance their children going to school.

When I look at what I want to do in the world, I know education lies at the heart of my work. However, we are faced with a vicious circle of circumstances that prevent the most vulnerable from getting an education and having a safe place to live.

We know that education is the key to employment, self-worth, confidence and empowerment. It is also within our knowledge that secondary school graduates can earn higher wages and contribute to their country's economic growth. Add in awareness of how this world is managed, about human rights and possibilities. Education, for all, means equality and understanding. With this knowledge and insight, we have decided to educate our family to have open minds.

Open minds and open hearts play a big part in my life, and I have made every possible effort, not only in my own life, but also in educating my children, to be more curious and adventurous. Open-mindedness for me is like a wheel of connected spokes, where each stands on its own and interacts with the other. I call it the equation of a balanced, open mind. Depending on who you are, and which approach to open-mindedness you choose, the equation's variables differ. My equation consists of Science, Education, Experience, Wellbeing, Personal Development, Will, Solidarity and Karma Yoga.

As an academic, I can appreciate the scientific approach to learning. Knowledge is power. When writing a scientific study, for example, the purpose, model, materials, method, results, discussion, conclusion, and rules are of the utmost importance. It is precisely because of these well-structured studies that we have made advancements in science and discovered what makes us human. We have been able to understand cause and connection, action and consequence. This knowledge has, to a large extent, propelled the human race forward.

In empirics and theory, an empirical study is made based on a sample of a more or less randomly selected population. You get a slice of reality, so that you can draw conclusions and base calculations on what might happen. This is all theoretical and subject to certain conditions. The theory is important because we have a framework to use. This means that others can interpret, draw conclusions or indeed criticise the findings. It is within the context of such scientific research that we have benefited from things like antibiotics and computers.

However, I think it is when science meets life experience that we can start to create a union called an "*open mind*". Our time in Australia, and our many other cultural adventures, as well as life itself, have given our family a valuable contribution to the possibility of an open mind.

Education is another aspect that helps to create an open, curious mind. You become accustomed to evaluating lots of information at college or university, in order to gain knowledge and grow from the experience. You are not just learning subjects. You are learning to think critically and learning to listen to others with differing perspectives. My university studies gave me a degree, proof that I have the potential to understand the course literature, process the facts and report this in the exams. Among other subjects, I studied economics, accounting, finance, business administration, business organisation and statistics, which are all very useful for an investor, as I later became. I am convinced that our financial foundation has allowed me to open my eyes. It has given us the freedom to travel to other corners of the world and listen to other people's stories.

A venture that really taught me a great deal, and has given me a euphoric sense of how things can work when everything synchronises together, was our women empowerment project in Costa Rica. It was like a textbook example of when the universal will merges with your own will. But I only realised that later, after completing my two-year coach training in psychosynthesis psychology. I also understood why I found my studies in a foreign language, and organisational psychology, more interesting than the university's economic subjects.

Roberto Assagioli is often referred to as the physician who founded Psychosynthesis during the 1920s, as a further direct development of Sigmund Freud's and C.G. Jung's work. In his literature, he emphasises the importance of being in touch with our will, and then developing it to take into account the prevailing circumstances, other people in our vicinity, our life purpose and finally allow it to align with "*Universal Will*". In other words, the state in which you find yourself, you allow yourself to be in the flow.

Other parts of the equation can be filled with things like Yoga, where there is also a framework, where the soul meets the body, and all the layers of you become one. It is with Yoga that you learn that you are not a machine. Yes, we are a human system that can be studied and theorised; however, we are also these many other multidimensional layers, unique to each one of us. Pour all of this into a vast melting pot, and the resulting union opens up new worlds. Add in a dash of curiosity and imagination, and we can create wonders.

Our women empowerment project, through vocational training and education in Costa Rica, results from the "*Universal Will*" combined with curiosity and flow. I am the first to admit that I think we should all follow our dreams, wherever they may take us, like the Elvis Presley song "*Follow Your Dream*". A dream without a structure is not likely to come true, although this is hard to digest for us visionaries. This is the main lesson I learnt during our time in Costa Rica. To "*go with the flow*" without getting lost requires proper planning and a strong will that is in harmony with your team's goal and your family members' intentions.

We took advantage of what we had learnt in Thailand about micro-credits, small loans to entrepreneurs and family providers, allowing them to become more self-sufficient and independent. We had watched many micro-enterprises flourish with help from these micro-loans. Many families could rebuild their lives after the tsunami disaster in Asia in 2004. In Costa Rica, there had not been a natural disaster, but there was a lot of poverty, oppression and injustice. Rich people took advantage of the poor, especially of the Nicaraguan immigrants fleeing from a military dictatorship. We once crossed the border into Nicaragua on a so-called "*visa run*" to extend our visas. We saw what a dictator can do to a beautiful country. So many people with no self-respect left, clinging to the roof of the car to make money from "*guarding*" the car, "*caring*" for our children or taking bribes to advance in the queue, stamping invalid passports and the like. There was nothing wrong with inventive creativity, if only the methods were more humane. We were seen as wandering wallets, and they saw themselves as lost souls. At least that was what their eyes reflected. Our experience was that pure cash often ended up in the wrong pockets, to be used for someone's abuse rather than for sustainability.

We asked ourselves if we would be able to swap money for education? It was worth a try to lend education instead of cash. But we were no teachers. How would we do this? That is when I came to think of my manicurist, Maria who had, just a few weeks before, asked me where our next philanthropic adventure would take place. She had reported her interest in volunteering next time. She was a teacher in manicure, pedicure and other beauty care. Of course! That is exactly what we wanted to do — vocational training and internships through microfinance. We made plans with Maria and booked a research trip to Costa Rica. One year later, the first group of women started their training with Maria in Huacas, Guanacaste, on the Pacific Coast.

Our move to Costa Rica was decided in consideration of all family members, at that time two adults, two pre-teen girls and a six-year-old boy. The small country between Panama in the south, and Nicaragua in the north, met all the criteria we had set. To give our children a broader view of the world, we needed to move relatively freely within the country. There should be good schools and the opportunity for meaningful leisure time. Language is an important factor for understanding a new culture, and being part of society. To give something back to the world we have received so much from, we need to live a comfortable family life and ensure that everyone is safe. It is next to impossible to meet everyone's wishes all the time, but the basic needs, such as safety, need to be prioritised. The country also needs to be relatively safe with excellent international schooling opportunities, and a playground for all ages, particularly if you enjoy surfing, diving and living close to water. On December 15th, we landed in San José, the capital of Costa Rica. Our plan was to buy a car and drive to the Pacific Coast to find a temporary home, a school and a location where we could start our project: a microfinance vocational school for women empowerment.

San José is a diverse network of poorly signposted streets. In the centre and the old town, many homeless people are wandering around with downcast eyes. The suburb of St Ana is the exception that confirms the rule. Here you will find lush gardens, picturesque neighbourhoods and a quieter atmosphere. We picked up our rental car and left for the Bed and Breakfast. Two small rooms, of which one had a working shower, would be our base for our first week in Costa

Rica. We needed a house, big enough for an active family, a pool or a view - preferably both. We also needed a car that could take us through flooded areas and bumpy roads, across lush vegetation and wetlands. We asked for a map at the reception, and a current daily newspaper. After reading through the ads, comparing them with the rental sites we had surfed and googled from Sweden, we quickly realised that what appeared to be a large selection, browsing the market from our comfortable sofa in Sweden, actually came down to very few opportunities for our family.

A few days later, we had bought a military green Range Rover Defender without any comfort whatsoever, but what appeared to be the perfect vehicle for our time in this country. It is not an understatement that the infrastructure is undeveloped in many places. This is offset by the exotic charm that the country offers. The whole country is like a national park, with its five different climate zones, along with fantastic plant and animal life. Although the country only occupies 0.1% of the world's total landmass, biodiversity accounts for as much as 5% of the world's animals and plants – something equivalent to between 500,000 and one million different species in flora and fauna.

In the middle of the jungle, we found it, our eagle's nest, with a view over the green mountains, and the Pacific Ocean meeting the sky on the horizon. At four o'clock in the morning, the howling monkeys wake up in the jungle tree crowns. At the same time, the mountains' silhouettes become visible. So do the early birds in our family. I would hear my son's heavy breaths as I walked past his bedroom, heading out to the sheltered balcony to roll out my Yoga mat in the soft morning air. The way that the sun coloured the sky pink on its way up behind the mountains always gave me strength. At that time of the morning, the moon would also leave traces of some calm feminine energy to balance it all out. On days like this, I find it is easy to be inspired and know how to do good.

It was here that we were honoured to meet Anna, and her husband Marlón. They were migrants from Nicaragua and worked as a housekeeper and gardener, in the rented house which became our home for almost a year. This is the situation in which many Nicaraguans find themselves within Costa Rica, as these are usually their only opportunities to earn a living wage. For a meagre salary, they were on duty 24 hours a day, as they guarded the house, which they were not allowed to leave at the same time. A worker must stay in the house all the time, because the risk of burglary is so high. Anna and Marlón told us that they had previously been blamed for a burglary where computers were stolen from the house. Compared to other Nicaraguan people in the country, their working conditions were good. Their salary was ridiculously low, but they did not work under slave-like conditions, like many of their compatriots. To share a household with staff is like trading service for privacy. It was not always pleasant to show your less flattering behaviours to someone outside the family, but the upside of the agreement was that Marlón kept our garden safe from rattlesnakes, and used the machetes to keep the vegetation in good shape. Anna made sure that we always had washed and ironed clothes, neatly placed in the closets, and knew how to remove the scorpions from their hiding places. Their knowledge was highly appreciated by us and worth a share of our space.

We rented premises free of charge from CEPIA, the non-profit organisation run by Laetitia, an entrepreneurial woman from Belgium, who founded a centre for children with tangled home relationships. At CEPIA, they learn about computers, do their homework, get therapy, build healthy relationships with buddies, and foremost they are given adult support. It's here that we found the first women for our project. A strange collection of women came together – some are divorced, poor, pregnant or even children themselves. So many of them brought with them tales of misery in the home, abuse, and drug abuse. Others were immigrant, illegal labour from Nicaragua, like Anna and Marlón, who had been poorly treated.

We tried to get Anna onboard on our micro-financed education project for women. In the beginning, she refused. After a while, we figured out that it must be her priest who would not allow such empowerment. It was clear he did not like either women, or Yoga, which he thought conflicted/competed with his religion. After a while, having seen me doing Yoga every morning at sunrise, Anna approached me one day and asked if it was possible to do Yoga only as a physical exercise, not as spiritual guidance. She was curious about how and if the manicure school could offer her a decent education. One thing led to another, and soon Anna was practising beauty care with us all.

I have such fond memories of how we created this school and touched lives, while educating our own children. At the start, they were homeschooled until we found the right place. The *International Bilingual School La Paz* was a paradise for learning. It was the kind of school I would have adored for myself, with an open Yoga Shala, where the sun and the breeze filled the space, as did the students' and teachers' morning meet and greet. On the walls, quotes like "*Be kind when possible. It's always possible*" are written. The Principal would greet every child and parent by their names at the parking lot in the morning. One thing that stands out is how the school welcomed our children into the school community. Beforehand, they had conducted investigations into what our children liked, what they were good at, their favourite movies, etc. On arrival one morning, the whole school gathered in the Yoga Shala and shared personalised information about their new friends. So humble. So welcoming. So kind.

We learned a lot about education during our time in Costa Rica. Including lots of fun stuff like our many visits to the surf mecca, Tamarindo. It was here that we all learned how to paddle out on our surfboards, turn towards the shore and paddle like crazy to catch the waves. Thanks to Diego, our Argentinian surf teacher who devotedly stood in the water for hours coaching us so well, we finally got it.

I learnt that I think best when it's morning. That moment, when the day is still like an unwritten sheet. New thoughts, ideas and perspectives come to me when the air is fresh, undisturbed, and the silence unbroken. It is essential to take advantage of the moment before the thoughts begin their cacophony, the mill wheels start to grind, and inner chaos arises. Five thirty every morning, I would set my alarm. It was more a safety measure than a necessity because the roaring (chattering?) monkeys woke me up at five o'clock anyway. Without waking the rest of the family, I would go out onto the balcony, roll out the Yoga mat, and keep a soft gaze on the horizon. It was so easy to find peace of mind and silence in the brain when the night sky began to change colour from black to dark blue. It was so simple to say yes to the approaching day, when the first butterfly of the morning sat down on the edge of the carpet as a sign of freedom. Meeting with women who need empowerment over pity was easier for me in an environment like this. I learned that I am more generous with both money, empathy and compliments when I feel comfortable myself.

In the same way that my father learned the hard way that you cannot treat daughters in the same way as you would treat your brothers or sons, I learned that you can't discuss instalment plans and loan terms with poor immigrants without education, as you might with the bank officer. I learned that challenges make you creative. Never take a "*no*" for an answer if it is about making a change for the better.

Above all, I cemented my desire to educate the world about injustice and became inspired to do good now because, whether you have children or not, you are always a role model. I have received the most important learning about the world and myself, from studying my own children. Children mirror your behaviours and reflect the best and worst parts of you. The things that trigger me negatively in my children's conduct are the things I dislike strongly about myself. I came to a place where I acknowledged and accepted that, although we are all one vibrationally, we are not all equal. Finally, our responsibility is to be good role models and learn the most significant lesson from children - how to accept each other.

Pause for thought

How would you feel if your child were denied the right to education? If they were cast aside because of a basic human characteristic, like race, gender or disability. What if you were a child who was denied it because instead, you had to support the family and bring in much-needed cash? Yet it happens. Many children in poverty, especially girls, do not have access to education. These aren't the only problems. Children are born in countries that do not have the funding, or properly educated people, to help them learn. Add to that no learning materials, a safe place to learn, or being in a country in conflict, and the nearest school is too far away for reasonable access.

These are things that many of us do not consider as we usher our children out of the house to go to school, or down to the kitchen table for homeschooling. Yet, we know that education benefits both individuals and society, and is one of the keys to sustainable development and reducing poverty.

According to Article 28 in the *Convention on the Rights of the Child* from November 1989, *The United Nations States Parties* recognises the right of all children to access education, regardless of race, gender or disability. The aim is to make primary education compulsory and freely available to all. In theory, many countries already offer this. However, in practice, this does not apply to all children, as poverty forces many families to make their children go out to work instead of studying. Even if there is a school at an accessible distance from home, many parents cannot afford the school literature, uniforms, shoes, or transport to get their children to and from school.

In Nepal, where I have focused much of my attention, schools are free, but the parents think the children contribute better by being in the rice fields, rather than at the school desk. Add to that the stigma around menstruation. What we find is that, 25% of the time, this prevents girls from going to school at all during this time of the month. As a result, many girls have little understanding of their natural bodily functions. When you combine that with schools forgetting to include it in their curriculum, you can see how tradition and culture sometimes prevent and hinder the next generation's access to knowledge.

In the same article, it is written that the development of different forms of secondary education, vocational training and higher education should be encouraged, as well as making available student grants or other financial assistance when needed. Yet, how can this be made available to all when many families have been locked into a cycle of poverty that has continued for generations?

What happens when it seems that everything is aligned for students to receive an education? Do they attend regularly? What about dropout rates? It's a vicious cycle. But, on the other hand, if they could acquire that much-needed education, imagine what that would do for poverty alleviation and reducing the incidence of child labour.

According to *UNESCO*, it is shocking to discover that there are 773 million illiterate adults worldwide, most of whom are women. One assumes that this cycle will also be perpetuated with the next generation of children.

Could you imagine what could happen with one child and one book? That child's imagination could be sparked, encouraging them to choose a career in perhaps the science or technical arena which, in turn, they use to support their country. Maybe they will go on to become teachers and share much-needed modern teaching methods.

I have no idea what your education was like, or what your thoughts may be, about the importance of education. But, still, I want to ask you if you do have young people around you, what do you want to pass on to them? What do you want them to know? How would you feel if they grew up to make a positive contribution to society? Proud, I bet.

Let's draw our attention back to the children facing a three-hour walk to the nearest school, or parents who simply cannot afford school uniforms or textbooks. Could the Covid-19 pandemic teach us anything? During this period, many schools switched to distance learning and homeschooling. Maybe this is an avenue for further exploration, especially for areas far from schools, or lacking a functioning infrastructure? Is it possible to imagine that a few computers and an adult mentor might be enough to start an educational revolution and a human evolution?

Chapter 9

Sexual exploitation is by far the most commonly identified form of human trafficking (79%), followed by forced labour (18%). [ix]

Truths and beliefs

"*Welcome to The Royal Orchid, Sir. How was your trip?*" The short journey from the airport to the hotel was over. The taxi door was opened by the hotel's piccolo in a red hat and vest. A brass wagon was rolled out by a concierge to take our luggage from the car to our room on the 17th floor, overlooking Bangkok's vibrant nightlife. This was the first stop on our three week vacation in Asia in the early '90s. My parents had given my brother and me the opportunity to experience a taste of Asia. Apart from Bangkok, we planned to visit the skyscrapers and the cross-over culture of Hong Kong, before it would be returned to China after more than 150 years under British rule, as well as Bali, which had just begun to be exploited with luxury hotels lined up along the strip of beaches.

My parents loved to travel. They wanted to give us the best life possible and invited us to share in their success. Above all, they wanted to share their travel experiences with my brother and me, for which I am eternally grateful. The investments they made in hard work, risk, and making their money work for them, were part of the reasons why we got to see the world. Many beautiful summer days were spent ensuring that the companies were able to support us all. I remember the disappointment in my mother's eyes when she had planned a wonderful day with the family in the garden, but instead, had to don her work suit and drive to their office in town. Mum loved being outdoors in the sun; however, my father's reward was trips to exotic places. Their belief was that long-distance travelling was the ultimate way to spend a vacation. I loved the excitement we felt browsing the travel magazines that adorned our coffee table. There was always such energy in anticipation of where we would be going next.

I still enjoy being at airports, hearing the announcements regarding delayed departures or immediate boarding. To me, this means freedom: a ticket to adventures and new horizons. Every tourist destination has its pride. A sunset. A beach. A waterfall. A tower. A special dish you definitely cannot live without.

When I travelled with my family, we were tourists in its proper sense — tourists who demanded pleasure, a glimpse of foreign cultures and, above all, experiences. Early on, my parents had embraced the trend of charter trips to the Canary Islands and other parts of southern Europe. It had to come with a guaranteed tan, which demonstrated our wealth. From there, they had sought out more exclusive arrangements offered by the tour operators who feasted on the desire of the

Swedish people to broaden their world view. When I look back, I can see how I inherited, and subsequently integrated, all of this into my own way of travelling. However, back then, in Bangkok, I was still a young spectator.

The concierge asked us how we wanted to spend our days in Thailand's capital. A guided tour of the floating market, perhaps? Dinner at one of the hotel's restaurants? Would we prefer him to make a reservation for us? So many decisions. While my parents were busy making all these choices, I explored the lobby, fascinated by the people around me. My eyes fell on a trio sitting at a table eating and chatting. The man who seemed to be European was chewing and talking while also gesturing with his arms and smiling to keep the conversation going as if his life depended on it. He made sure that the dialogue never ended because silence, I sensed, would mean failure. Opposite him sat two girls, who appeared to be Asian, their hands placed in their laps for the most part. They did the rocking/shaking nod with their heads every now and then, which means "*yes*", and smiled.

Back then, I was just curious, and my people-watching in the hotel lobby meant nothing. Many years later, during our year of volunteering after the tsunami disaster in Thailand, I would recall this scene and realise that there was much more to it than an innocent dinner party as I had believed at the time.

In 2007, I was invited to a home for women and children with HIV in Phuket, Thailand. The women's stories brought me to a world of extreme poverty and misery, where abuse and sexually transmitted diseases were commonplace. One woman had married a man who lent her, free of charge, to business acquaintances when it suited his business. Her nose jewellery gleamed as she turned her head away, in shame, when she showed me the skin lesions on her arms, caused by AIDS. Another woman had grown up as one of seven siblings, with an alcoholic father. The fastest way to put food on the table for her siblings was for her to take temporary jobs at the Go-Go bars. Sometimes she was expected to stand at a pole, stripped of her clothing, dancing to western pop music. Her naked body served as part of a sex tourist's foreplay, while he was choosing which girl he would bring to his hotel room to make his wet dreams come true. Sometimes she was the girl a man wanted as his toy. After having worked in this way for some time, she understood how a woman gets pregnant, and she now has a daughter who was lucky enough not to be born with HIV.

Through their stories, the Thai women invited me into a life that was completely alien to me and of which I had no experience. It did not scare me. I had no fear. What I had, was a great number of questions that would subsequently support the implementation of ideas that had started to take shape inside my head. I knew it would take a long time to bring everything I wanted to do to fruition. Once I'd heard the stories, and they were in my heart, I couldn't turn my back and continue my life as if these women never existed, and as if these abuses had never been committed. It's funny how things catch you and, in that instant, you gain a knowing. I did not know precisely how I would do things, only that I would spend a large part of the rest of my life putting an end to this horrendous oppression.

After one year in Thailand, I learned to interpret the different smiles. Rarely did I meet smiles that were honestly happy and friendly. More often, I was greeted by the smile intended for tourists – like the henna artist that I'd previously met in Dubai. The smiles I got from the women I interviewed hid unbelievable truths and nightmares.

The paradox was that, just as they hid their truths behind their smiles, so did I. My smile was my protection. I used it to stop my mind from racing with thoughts as my body would be gripped by uncomfortable feelings. I'd always say I was fine, and wonder why I was struggling despite no apparent trauma in my past. Behind my smile, I hid my emotional eating. Like the depravity I was witnessing, I felt almost sinful for hiding my truths – just as they did theirs, but I believed this is what I must do.

Behind Thailand's depravity lies an incredible culinary experience with many delicious, spicy or very spicy dishes. With our own chilli bush in the garden, we tried many experiments in the kitchen. The "*Tom Yum Goong*" soup smelt wonderfully of lemongrass, chilli, lime juice and fresh shrimps. "*Som Tum*", a green papaya salad tossed in a clear lime, garlic- and chilli dressing was divine. When we searched for more inspiration for cooking, seafood and live jazz music, we discovered a restaurant nestled in a hillside with a beautiful view of the ocean. The *Ratri Restaurant* became one of our favourite watering holes in the chaotic world of bars, massage studios, and tourists ferried around in the motorised tricycle "*tuk-tuk*" taxis.

I do not live by many mottoes, but the old adage, "*There cannot be good without bad*", forms part of an idea that there must always be a balance. It felt as if this was a prophecy coming true because, while I was enjoying life, the little oyster changed my view of this world and of myself. Late in the evening, my body began to react to the bacteria that the oyster I was enjoying had carried. It started to attack my digestive system with its poison. The result was that, for many days, my body refused to keep any food or drink down. The parasite made a nest inside me, and did not want to leave. As she settled in, I became thinner and thinner. I began to lose my hair and saw with delight how the bathroom scale displayed lower and lower numbers. The hair did not bother me. After all, I lived in a tropical place where having a sun-tanned, slim body was all anyone needed.

Having had problems with emotional eating for much of my life, this was a gift from heaven. I became almost as slim as I had always desired, which allowed me to move around the beach without feeling ashamed, or pulling my stomach in. I felt that I had been gifted an almost perfect body. The added bonus was that I did not feel weak. In my distorted view of myself, I had believed that I had been carrying too many extra kilos when we arrived in Phuket. I had arrived with the belief that I was "*the chubby girl with a strong bone structure and fat thighs*". Looking back, I can see this was not the truth, only a perception of my self-image. Like so many women, I had accepted the media's picture of what a successful woman looks like. I'd pored over images of women with beautiful smiles, on a symmetrical face, placed on a slender yet curvy body. All evidence that she followed a sensible calorie controlled diet, along with a busy work-out schedule. Her only task was to please the eye of the beholder.

After a while, my appetite betrayed me and came back, but not my body's ability to keep it in. Eventually, I existed on a diet consisting of vegetables and fruits. Finally, luckily, I got the recommendation to go to an Ayurvedic healing centre that had cleansing and rehabilitation programmes for those who needed it, following heart surgery, cancer and stress-related illnesses. This was my first contact with Ayurvedic medicine, and I became hooked. Ayurveda sees a person holistically, and understands that they need to heal according to their own unique genetic information and needs. This was indeed a revelation that would prove to support the desperately needed healing of my soul.

"*Why are you burning your candle at both ends*?" I wasn't paying much attention, as the head of the centre asked the question while reading my pulse. It took a moment to realise that the question was for me. ME?! It had never crossed my mind that I was living this way, at least while we were submerged in living in this paradise. Admittedly, this was a new environment, and we were witnessing people who had suffered severe losses through the tsunami. Yet, somehow the work we were doing and which consumed my heart and many waking hours, didn't seem like work. However, here was someone who, for the first time, challenged my truths and beliefs. Then came my prescription - fasting for ten days, with water, psyllium husk and clay, designed to cleanse the intestinal system and rid me of the parasite which had been enjoying her holiday in my body. Each morning began with Yoga and meditation, followed by bowel rinsing, rest and massage. We often sat in a circle sharing our fasting experiences, or pulled cards from a deck of spiritual messages, that always seemed appropriate for where we found ourselves and our experiences.

It all began well, except that my motivation for action had left me, and it seemed like I wasn't achieving a lot. By day five, I started to long for food, and by day six, I wanted to kill the Yoga teacher when she ordered us all out on "*a little walk*" of two hours up a steep mountain path and back. On the sixth evening, we were served a so-called "*liver cleanse*", consisting of pressed garlic cloves, lime juice and olive oil. The only way to drink it was to hold my nose and swallow down the five decilitres of the greasy mixture without breathing. The next day I was so sick that I could not get out of bed. The poison had started to leave my body, and it felt as if I had emptied the bar the night before. Stefan pulled me out of bed, drove me back to the centre and forced me to do Yoga. After the Yoga session, I felt better. During meditation, I witnessed a kind of clear-sightedness I had never experienced before. I felt gratitude without guilt. I gave myself permission to be without doing, and it was fine. I discovered a truth about myself that helped shape my beliefs about what I could achieve in the world. It was mind-blowing. Only when you hit rock bottom, and the ugly truth helps you to shed your protective skin, do you realise who you are and who you are becoming. I came into contact with something remarkable in my heart. I felt thankful for so much. I discovered I was brave, and I realised that I am capable of anything if I hold the belief that I can.

On the day that we were ordered to go on a walkabout up the long steep hilly mountain path, something was aroused in me. I knew nothing was impossible. There and then, I knew I could and would make a difference, because something quite profound had changed within me. That something was that I had arrived in Thailand to support the rebuild, and I knew I was leaving with a mission successfully accomplished.

I still look back and reflect with amazement that we had come to Thailand to help to rebuild the infrastructure after the tsunami disaster. Our role was to administer microcredits and small loans to entrepreneurs and family providers, so that they could rebuild their lives. I left the country with a mission, commitment, and dream tucked away in my luggage. That mission was to stop human trafficking for sexual purposes.

It seems incredible that I didn't realise the full extent of the sex industry offerings, yet I just knew I had to do something. Nor was I aware of the considerable number of people still being tricked and forced to survive by selling their bodies. This industry, I came to discover, is extremely lucrative. A human body can be sold countless times before it is considered trash and ready to be dumped. It started to dawn on me that, as long as there is a demand for sexual services and people willing to pay for sexual services, there will be a trade for these purposes.

I began to ask questions. I started to look behind the facades. Behind the smiles, I met story after story that began to form a pattern of women's fate, with one common denominator. This was advocated by men, who wanted their bodies, not their intelligence and friendship, but just for their sexual value. As the veils began to fall, I realised more and more that the way in which people treat others says a lot about who they are and their truths and beliefs. This also, naturally, says a lot about why there is a demand for human trafficking.

The women who allowed me to interview them will never leave me. Their footprints will forever be my heart. What I learned, going forward, is that while there are different women with different faces, behind the masks, the stories are all the same. All etched with betrayal and sadness. Humanity,

I have concluded, is littered with shadows that need the light shining into them.

While thinking of these women, I am reminded of a trip to Dubai many years before. It made me realise how far I have come on this journey, how my eyes have been further opened to the truth, and how my beliefs about the world have changed.

In my mind's eye, I can still see the henna tattoo beginning to take shape on my hand. The veiled woman held my hand in a firm but soft grip - so feminine, sensual yet so determined. Her beautiful eyes were surrounded by thick eyeliner, and the dense eyelashes were covered with copious amounts of mascara. Something told me that the woman was not of Arab origin. It was not really her appearance that was the cause of my question, but rather that I was restless and had difficulty sitting still. Curious as ever, I asked, "*Are you from Dubai?*" She froze for a second, which resulted in a notch in the pattern that represented a winding plant with broad stalk leaves. "*The Philippines*", she answered briefly and continued to paint flower petals along my forearm. The ensuing conversation took place between a hard-working woman and a naive tourist. The woman who made my henna tattoo was one of the thousands of migrant workers in Dubai, whose passport had been seized by the so-called employer, and who had not seen her daughter in two years. Her daughter was being raised by her grandparents at home in the Philippines. This contrasted with my life as my daughters were with me, and playing in one of the hotel's pools, 50 metres away from us. What I believed about happiness was that the family needed to be together to enjoy ourselves. I felt a sting of disgust at myself but had forgotten all about it by lunchtime. I simply accepted it and carried on with my life.

The services I enjoyed were an intrinsic part of how my family expected their holidays to be. The people looking after me had a job, which was to serve me, and I accepted that this was the norm. I remember my relatives telling me that it was better to travel to faraway places, be a good tourist and pay for the services, rather than leaving them jobless and poor.

This "*we and they*" way of thinking is now something I used to be part of. While I agree with my family on one level, the reality is much more complex. Morally we cannot clear our consciences only by spending some money in a place we will soon leave and forget about by the following Monday. As tourists, we can support the local economy, for sure, but there is more that we can do.

Now I believe in making an impact by asking those uncomfortable questions, such as "is this hotel built by migrant workers, and if so, where do they come from? How is their salary paid? Is the fruit at the breakfast buffet locally produced? Which items on the menu are organically grown? Why does your hotel offer pornography movies on demand? Could you please show me the hotel's Code of Conduct?" and so on. I consider myself a more conscious traveller now, but I still have a long way to go. I continue to make naive choices, and unconscious mistakes, such as buying avocado and kiwi for breakfast, when I know all too well that they are grown far from Sweden.

As I write this, I want to question myself, my truths, and my beliefs once again. Another memory creeps in. Who am I to judge the man, sitting with two Thai girls in Bangkok? From what I now know, I believe he was a predator, and the two girls were his victims. What if the truth is different? What if he believes that he has to pay for sex because society taught him that women are here to please men? What if he thinks the only way to intimacy is through paid services? I don't know, do you? Whatever his motives, the girls, I still believe, were the vulnerable ones. I feel in my heart that these were two victims preyed upon by traffickers, lured and brainwashed into prostitution. What are their beliefs? Maybe they considered it better to give men some fake love occasionally, rather than working under adverse conditions in a factory 18 hours per day? It is a complex situation, each serving the other, but what did they really want for their lives?

When I consider the intricacies of this way of living, it brings up so many questions in me. Once again, I say to myself, who am I to tell anyone that the way they live their lives is wrong or that you should never watch porn because it destroys society, relationships and your brain? I have read scientific evidence and have seen proof that frequent porn consumption can lead to addiction. This addiction feeds a craving for more violent material for the consumer to become aroused. I am sure that, as they are lured in further, their belief system will tell them that this is acceptable. Naturally, I haven't watched this pornography and nor would I want to. The truth is that I find this abhorrent. By way of understanding, I have listened to the stories from former addicts, and have studied the previously mentioned reports.

No one will change my mind or belief system, which maintains that sex against someone's free will is rape. No amount of describing it in other ways, such as ethical porn, will change the fact that it is still porn. Ethical porn is pornography that, I am told, is made consensually, treats performers with respect, and pays everyone fairly for their work. All of this is based on a mutual agreement between the porn actors and the film team, with acceptable working conditions and legislation and security measures so that minors cannot enter the porn site. These sites require an ID to enter, which details the user's credentials, just as you would for a bank account. The problem is that so many people want to make money off the back of trafficked children and young porn consumers that it will never happen. I can only wonder why they do not care. And if I do not care, I am making it easy for the traffickers and the sex industry to continue. I have to believe that I can make a difference in all areas of this insidious industry.

Yet, what is "*truth*" and what is the relationship between truth and beliefs? For a true proposition to be known, it must be a justified belief. This is what many philosophers agree on. Could a proposition be true unless we know it to be true? According to Aristotle's theory of truth, true or false are of three main kinds: sentences, thoughts, and specific objects, whose nature is neither mental nor linguistic.

This means you don't always see the truth, or what people are hiding, unless you are a mind reader or a clairvoyant. What lies behind what we see, we can only guess. Why is this relevant for the continuing story? Because your beliefs have shaped you and, from your perspective, they have designed your truth. If you and I were to change places and continue this story, it would be a whole different chapter.

It is all about perspectives. Truths and beliefs are so intricately interwoven. I love this quote because it cleverly takes you through what happens in an instant:

"Your beliefs become your thoughts,

Your thoughts become your words,
Your words become your actions,
Your actions become your habits,
Your habits become your values,
Your values become your destiny."
Mahatma Gandhi

Believing you cannot change is a myth. Once your eyes are no longer covered, some ugly truths will be revealed. You cannot put the truth back in its box. You either continue to turn a blind eye, or you act. What will you do?

You use your beliefs to understand and navigate your world. Remembering that the body's prime objective is safety, you also use your beliefs to keep yourself safe. And the scariest of all is that we try to preserve our beliefs and guard them carefully. Your beliefs also dictate what you consider to be possible or achievable.

Your beliefs operate on autopilot, and you may not even notice that they could possibly be a bit faulty. That is, until someone reveals their personal truth to you, which could open up a whole new perspective.

Thoughts contain your ideas, opinions, and beliefs about yourself and the world around you. They enable you to form your values and behaviours, which progress to actions and lead to habits. They colour your point of view and the perspective that you hold. In simple terms, thoughts are shaped by life experiences and what you see, feel and hear.

Thoughts influence your reality. What you think directly influences how you feel and how you behave. So if you think you're a failure, you'll feel like a failure. Then, you'll act like a failure, which reinforces your belief that you must be a failure. When you feel like a failure, you will often perpetuate the actions that lead to physical symptoms, such as anxiety, or perhaps it will manifest in a dis-ease.

Once you have drawn a conclusion about yourself, you're likely to do two things: look for evidence that reinforces your belief, and discount anything that runs contrary to that. I do this with my belief that I look fat on the beach, and my belief that porn cannot possibly be ethical.

I was once told that porn and prostitution can be part of women empowerment. The speaker argued: Why should it be less ethical to expose your vagina being penetrated by a penis online than to be an influencer, pretending to like the brand you get best paid to promote? For me, the difference is obvious, the influencer has the power to change brands if they are not well-paid, or if another brand lures them away. I am not so sure about performers in the porn industry. Whilst I do not have intimate knowledge around the inner workings, my heart tells me that most of these performers cannot pick and choose their porn brand so easily, or influence their co-actors, clothes and salary. What I am certain about is that empowerment is not about being oppressed and forced to perform acts of sex day after day.

Naturally, there are those in the porn industry who claim that this is a great job, which pays the bills and enables them to afford things they might not have been able to in another role. I guess if you can command $1000 a scene and get 100 scenes a year, it could be worth your while for a time. But empowered? Never.

Would I agree to perform in a couple of porn movies per week instead of working 24/7 to support my children and never spend time with them because of my work? No. According to my non-scientific investigation and beliefs, I think the porn industry's conditions are formed by criminality, grey zones, limited choices and oppression.

Again, your selection of choices depends on your life circumstances, and your beliefs. Do you know where yours have come from? The ones that tell you that you are a loser, a failure, unlikable, unlovable, or incapable. The beliefs that prevent you from doing your best, being your best self and doing good in your world. My opinion is that when we allow ourselves to shine and be awesome, genuinely amazing people, we make the best of choices. So let us choose to *Do Good, Feel Good* and be as inspiring as we can — every day.

Pause for thought

You might not realise it, but we are all part of the demand that drives Modern Slavery, in which Human Trafficking plays a great part. As a business, have you checked your supply chain? Many businesses are simply not aware of the *Modern Slavery Act*, let alone realise that they need to ensure transparency in their production. The biggest problems arise where there is a complex global supply chain. It is incumbent on businesses to ensure that they are not unwittingly involved in exploitative labour.

But what of you, as a consumer, have you looked into what goes into the production of your products? Our actions as consumers matter. How can you tell if your tomatoes or jeans come from a reputable business? As we increase the demand for cheaper products and services, exploitation is more likely to occur.

I read that "It is estimated that in 2019 there were 40 million people in the world living in conditions of slavery or working under forced or compulsory conditions. [x] This means that a part of your business or life is, in some way, contributing to this.

That's a sobering thought, isn't it? Something that you buy could be contributing to this industry, either directly or indirectly. What you need to know is that human trafficking is not a problem of The Global South. It is a global problem. It's our problem.

If you haven't booked your holiday yet, where do you fancy going? Did you know that there is a big trade in sex tourism destinations? Of course, in many of these places, prostitution is not illegal, but that doesn't change the fact that many of the girls have been forced into these jobs.

Interestingly Sweden, where I am from, makes it illegal to buy sex, but not *to sell the use of one's own body for such services*. The *Swedish Prostitution Act* has proven to be one of the most important tools against prostitution. It is not a moral law, but a way of curbing the modern slave trade. In Sweden, about 200 sex buyers are arrested every year. This is not a high figure per se, but the law has a strong preventive effect. The Swedish Police have good knowledge of the prostitution industry and make a strong contribution to changing attitudes.[xi] I often hear the age-old argument that women work in prostitution of their own free will. I wonder when people will realise that the inviting smile that a prostitute offers is no more authentic than the Rolex replicas sold on tourist beaches around the world?

There are only four core reasons why a person ends up in prostitution. These are poverty, drug abuse, mental illness or previous abuse. Grey zones exist, of course, but it is not the extremely rare cases of women who have become more independent since selling their bodies that should be highlighted here. Instead, it is time to kill the myth of the happy whore. I do not think she exists.

Let's leave the beach and think about Christmas. Have you been thinking about the toys you will get for your children? How would you feel about asking, "*Is this toy produced by children*?" before purchasing. Hopefully, this simple question will lead to a rewarding discussion in the store. Although some staff may not be aware of their company's *Modern Slavery Policy*, if they do not want to talk about this or are uninterested, there is probably a reason to walk away.

Another way to raise the issue and show that you, as a customer, caring about sustainability, is to ask, "*What is your company's corporate social responsibility policy and Modern Slavery Policy? Where can I read about it?*" Many businesses have these on their website but, if they don't, you can decide with your feet and return when they do. Making this kind of request will also arouse the employees' desire to question their company's policies and behaviour.

I hope that, in the future, more businesses and consumers will become aware of this, and only work with sustainable companies with sound policies. Of course, the knock-on effect for businesses is that they will attract conscious employees and customers. However, the problem remains that there will still be demand from low-income earners, who look for the less expensive sustainable alternatives.

Acts such as the *Modern Slavery Act* go some way to regulating this, but we all need to demand legislation that regulates environmental crime, corruption, modern slave labour and slave-like working conditions, sexual exploitation for commercial purposes and, not least, child labour and so-called child sex trafficking.

You may be questioning how did it get to this? It's quite simple. After all, we are only human. To long for something to fill our emptiness is a part of the human condition. Retail therapy to sop up unhappiness is well documented. People believe that they can buy, albeit very short-lived, happiness by having yet more clothes. When we buy stuff, the brain's reward system is activated. Then when the dopamine rush subsides and reality kicks in, the desire for more bursts through. More of the stimuli would be required to reach the same effect. So naturally, you will need more products and services to satisfy your needs. You are, in effect, wired for pleasure.

Becoming consciously aware is the first step. So let's take that now and ask more questions.

Chapter 10

"Happy, healthy people don't buy sex." [xii]

Choices

Is there such a thing as a free choice, or even the freedom to make choices? I know my answer to that question, but the true answer lies in everybody's individual faith, belief or conviction. It also lies in where they live, their culture, upbringing and a myriad of other criteria.

    I have the luxury to choose between spending time with my children, writing this book, working on developing my real estate business together with my close family, or going to Yoga. This tells you that I have a lot of freedom with my personal choices. I am free to decide what I do with my time. I have this freedom because of many factors, yet I often feel like a spoiled brat. It sometimes feels, and perhaps looks to the casual observer, that I do not need to work hard, but I choose to. My personality drives my inner stress, and I get burned out quickly, have panic attacks and cry a lot. Perhaps not something I should confess to; however, I choose to reveal all of myself. Every day I have to tell myself to be consciously aware of how I make my choices, that I have choices, and to appreciate them. I even have the luxury of making some unwise choices. If you give me lemons, I can make lemonade in my fancy kitchen, or pour in a generous helping of vodka, put an umbrella in it, and make my way through the bottle, while I muse on whatever is on my mind. But, what is the point of my musing?

If you are living in a democracy, you can cast your vote when the elections come. You also have the right to have an opinion and the freedom to express yourself, as long as you are not threatening anyone, doing anything illegal, immoral or unethical. If you live in a society that offers freedom of speech, equality and justice, think yourself lucky, because many have no choice or even a voice. If your country's leader is a dictator, your options might be somewhat limited. No matter where you are, you will still make decisions based on what you believe, or perhaps based on what you have been taught. My choices always seemed important and necessary. It was as if there was no other option. I had to do these things. However, the more I travelled, the more I realised how privileged I was to have choices.

One of our recent choices saw us travelling to a beautiful destination for a family holiday. We didn't know at the time what the consequences would be, or how this simple choice could lead to both joy and shadow. I've already said that, because we live in a democracy, we have a lot of freedom to choose how to spend our time. In February 2020, we decided to travel to Cervinia. Cervinia is situated in the mountainous autonomous region of northwestern Italy. Call to mind a picturesque village nestled in the Aosta valley. Even if you haven't been or heard of it, you will have heard of the

Matterhorn and know that this is a skiing region. With our usual excitement, we packed and headed for what was sure to be another adventure for our clan. Little did we know that this escapade would affect our future and our choices.

It was my choice to go to Italy. We had been there four years previous, and that trip ended in disaster. I will never forget the last morning when I came down to the breakfast room, where the mood was as heavy as a dense fog. Some words had been carelessly spoken, which smothered and hurt us like a negligent statement. We went home in tears. My intention for this holiday was that we would heal that old wound. Before leaving, I held a vision of this beautiful place and of healing our wounds. I wanted to travel back to undo the harm and create better memories. Our holiday was able to lick the wounds of the past, and we were so happy.

Within no time at all, the holiday was over, and we were on our way back to Stockholm. I love to look out of the plane window and lose myself in the lights and signs on the runway, becoming more evident as the plane approaches the landing. Followed by the familiar bang when the landing gear was lowered, after the announcement "*Cabin crew prepare for landing*" had been made. Taking my eyes back to my iPad, I read the last lines of the BBC News article about the coronavirus outbreak.

The statement told me that the coronavirus, COVID-19, was affecting 83 countries and territories around the world… Earlier that morning, the Swedish government had advised that no further action was to be taken, as long as you did not have any symptoms, or were arriving directly from China, where the outbreak began. I noted that Japan was the only country where all schools closed down due to the pandemic.

This found me shocked and curious, but I gave it no more thought as we diligently disembarked and made our way home.

We soon learned of the consequences of our sojourn. Our children attended an international school, which meant that many families were regular international travellers. Given this, our school decided that all students who had spent time in the most affected regions, including Northern Italy, should be quarantined. This would typically not mean any trauma for our family, because we have a lot of free working hours, and a flexible routine Monday to Friday. However, being a family of six people of varying ages and interests, you can imagine that no matter how many free hours we might perceive that we had, we always seemed to fill them with various tasks, vital or not.

No school for either our sixteen or five-year-olds, meant that it was now up to us to make sure their days were filled with meaningful activities. I was struck by a myriad of conflicting thoughts and emotions. My conscience was playing tricks on me, because all I wanted to do was to sit down and write my book. After a week of fresh air, skiing, good food and entertainment, I longed to dig into the literature I had collated on human trafficking, gather my employees, and change the world. In my mind, I had expected to get at least six hours a day to spend on work, writing, Yoga, training and time for myself. Despite having had the privilege of spending a lot of time with each of my amazing kids through the years, where we enjoyed playing, studying, working out or just hanging out, right now, I desired some me time. Reflecting on our choices, I felt trapped, because my opportunities were limited, because I decided to spend the holiday in Lombardy, Italy.

Another unexpected event took place in the early '90s. I was faced with a choice I did not realise was crucial at that time. I had been working for the Ministry off Foreign Affairs in Stockholm for a couple of years, and loved the feeling of being in the wonderful turmoil of the world's events. Surrounded by many intelligent colleagues, who worked hard and were focused, was a delight. The news from the World Bank and the UN was discussed at meetings, and I felt important despite not having an executive role. However, I wanted more and recognised that, to have a great career in the diplomatic world, it helps to have one or two degrees from a University. I was overjoyed that my decision to study economics at the University of Uppsala was highly appreciated by those in authority. The plan was to come back in three or four years and get a job with more responsibility. My boss gave me clear signs that he wanted me back, and I wondered if I could complete my education in a shorter period? Back then, I did not really understand the great opportunity which had been presented to me. Our family business grew quickly while I was studying. My father was proud that our company was being recognised as an organisation to count on, with potential to become a dominant player in the real estate industry. I made a decision that was, in hindsight, based on my belief that I wasn't capable of changing the world at a higher diplomatic level. Looking back, I feel that I did not give myself the opportunity of having the United Nations and World Bank within reach. I literally threw an outstanding career in the bin, together with my chances of having a real impact on society. Also in the bin were the exciting talks about strategies for sustainable investments for the future, with the expected outcome of creating a better world.

We are always being guided. If I had started on that diplomatic journey, and chosen that as my path, I might have missed the miracle moment of meeting a newborn's gaze, or meeting an innocent human being untainted by life. I might never have held a small hand in mine, or met a curious smile in the morning. I may never have had the joy of open arms as I approached. It is humbling to discover that children can teach you, in their innocence, the hardest lessons. I recall one of my fantastic children telling me that "*It doesn't feel like I've had my mother for the past two years*". What she said taught me that we need to nurture our meaningful relationships before we go out and try to make a difference for those further away. This showed me that if I work around the clock on changing the world, it means very little if I am not present to my own family's needs.

Over the years, I have reflected back on my choice not to continue with my career at the Ministry of Foreign Affairs. I have questioned myself many times. On my deathbed, I hope to say with conviction that it was the right decision, based on my values and beliefs. When I am leaving this Earth, I hope my soul reminds me that I created change and achieved my goal.

No matter how many regrets we might have, my point is that there is no such thing as a bad choice. There is only the choice you make in the moment. Naturally, what you select depends on your values, beliefs, experiences and your current circumstances at the time. To walk on thin ice in springtime can be a really bad choice, especially if you do not want to be sucked under the ice and have your life terminated. What about hitting out to defend yourself? I've taught my children that hitting someone is a bad choice, but what happens if they need it as a method of protection? The law will naturally want to know why they took this line of defence. No matter how many obvious choices there might be for any given situation, I believe that it always comes back to the point of our truth. Having a strong moral compass as your guide will always point you in the right direction.

Knowing that the path you are walking is your true life path is a question many people have asked. Where am I going? Why am I here? What is it that I am meant to be doing in this lifetime? It's a very human thing to desire certainty, to know for sure that this is the right way for us. We think that we should know where we are going. We set goals and take action and do stuff, and often find ourselves frustrated and angry that things are not going according to plan. Things keep happening, and soon all your best-laid plans become a horrible mess. I have learned over the years that plans are good, as long as you allow your heart some latitude to change them. After all, a plan is merely a suggestion, isn't it? Is it always our choice which path we head down? It is implicit that every choice leads to another one.

When I observe animals or small children, I am amazed at the simplicity of their choices. Sniff this, put this in your mouth and see how it tastes. They may decide to run, play or simply sleep. Something may happen, and they head off in a natural and unconscious direction, simply because it's the right choice in the moment. Why do we complicate things as we get older? I feel jealous that animals and small children have this apparent free will to wander wherever they desire, compared to others who, it seems, have choices thrust upon them.

All my life, I believed I had been forced into a bodysuit that was not mine. I hadn't chosen to look like this, yet this was me. I don't remember anyone asking me if I wanted to be Swedish or grow up in Sweden, yet here I was. Of course, I know that no matter the circumstances of birth and body, we can choose to be more. Making healthy food choices, working out and doing what I can for human rights, and against poverty and oppression, feels right. I choose to feel good so that I can do good, which makes me feel good.

This morning my choice was to skip my beloved Yoga class to give myself time to write. This is not something I often do, but after three mornings of work and no Yoga, my head started to show the familiar signs of stress, making it hard to concentrate. My inner voice could clearly hear my Yoga master's advice. "*Do not dwell in the past or worry about the future. Do your practice now, and the rest will come.*"

It's sometimes easier said than done, as my mind relaxed and was flung back into a memory from a Yoga workshop.

It's in the cafè I see him, as he is looking down at his coffee, preparing to take a bite of his sandwich. I wonder what he is thinking about, and what he would say to me if he was aware of my presence. Looking up, he catches my eye and chooses to use his voice to make contact and show he wants to be a part of our community. "*I am from Argentina, temporarily based in Sweden for a job,*" he tells me, explaining his Spanish accent. I could sense that he was a traveller seeking adventure. You could also tell that he was an extrovert or perhaps had learned how to be one, as he was the one that was always prepared to start a conversation or share a story. I have met his type many times before, the kind of person who seems incapable of being embarrassed, and who seems so at home no matter where they are. Because he seems to have no fear, I am intrigued and want to learn more. As our conversation continues, I am reminded of another soul that I wanted to learn from.

I met Adriana in Costa Rica. She made me realise what it is like to have limited choices in life. When I think of Adriana, I am reminded to choose joy. She chose to value the gifts that she had been given, rather than lamenting the things, like the voice Adriana wished she could have. Adriana was deaf and dumb. She spoke with her eyes and could hear with her hands. To meet her gaze is like watching a movie and listening to a story simultaneously — such strong expressions. So much to tell. We met for the first time in 2011. I learned that she grew up in Guanacaste, on Costa Rica's Pacific coast. Adriana lived not far from the sea in a small house constructed of sheet metal, clay and boards. She was the firstborn of many children. She joined our empowerment programme for women, which you will have read about in Chapter x. This training gave her more choices, more freedom, and a chance to earn her own money.

Coming back from my journey into my memories, my email pinged. It was an online petition forwarded by a friend. The call was to sign a petition against PornHub's idea of offering porn for free during the Covid-19 pandemic. Sitting back to take it in, I felt like someone had written the world a bizarre message. *"Dear Porn Consumer, now that you are spending a lot of time at home from work or school, take this opportunity to watch as much porn as possible. Your brain's reward centre will love this gift, and unbeknown to you, we will have installed a trigger so that pornography is seen as a treat for having to endure such hard times. Over time this will cause you to demand rougher and more violent porn. In the end, you will demand darker and darker material. Even though this wonderful service is being offered to you free of charge, we will ultimately make lots of money from you. Once you are hooked, you will no longer have free will or free choice. When we start to charge again, you will pay dearly for your choice to masturbate over our site."*

Pornhub and similar sites know that offering this kind of stuff for free will massively increase their user base. They do not care that they are shamelessly taking advantage of human pain and suffering. Speaking out on this point, Dr Gail Dines, founder of the organisation, *Culture Reframed,* and one of the most well-known researchers into the porn industry, responded with, "*For too long pornography has been framed as a moral issue, but from over forty years of empirical research, we know that it is an issue of harm. Pornhub is in the business of commodifying and monetising violence against women and children. There is no place for Pornhub in a world committed to sexual equality, dignity, and social justice.*"

You might recall the brief description of how our brains are wired, when it comes to addiction, from Chapter 3. It happens so easily and quickly. Wendy Seltzer, an attorney at Yale Law School, explains simply: once porn consumers get hooked, they'll want more and more. "*Seeing [free porn] just whets their appetite for more,*" Seltzer says. "*Once they get through what's available for free, they'll move into the paid services.*"

You might wonder how pornographers can be so sure? The answer is right there inside the brain. Repeated consumption of porn causes the brain to literally rewire itself. It triggers the brain to pump out chemicals and form new neural pathways, leading to profound and lasting changes in the brain. And so, new choice pathways are created.

You could argue that it is a choice whether to consume porn or not. But, once those chemicals take hold, it is hard to change. Addiction is a hard taskmaster that demands a lot from you. Through that demand, the choices for the people on the other side of the equation are limited. It is because the most marginalised, vulnerable, and defenceless people in the world will have the course of their lives forever changed, and their choices restricted, that I did not think twice before signing the petition and sharing it everywhere I could.

I started this journey understanding that prostitution was not just the result of a lack of choice. It is also the effect, outcome and consequence of poverty, drug addiction, sexual abuse and mental illness. Even if many sex workers would argue that they do this from free will, I'm curious about why anyone would make a choice to let someone use their body for money. That probably sounds naive. Of course, I know why. Just like I do not know every sex worker, porn film performer or brothel owner in the world, I remain convinced that no one would rent out their vagina to be abused in this way.

Equally, I am shocked by those who want to call prostitution "*women's empowerment*". My guess is that they have probably not tried the profession themselves. They have had other choices available. Yet, they still declare that this is an honourable choice, just like those who claim that prostitution is the oldest profession on Earth and is, therefore, somehow acceptable because it's been around for a long time.

In my opinion, this is the world's oldest form of oppression. Or, like a former "pimp" from Romania puts it, "Since no girl or woman sells sex because they like it, it is not a mutual business transaction with two content actors. Therefore, prostitution should be called by its correct label: Rape."

I'll leave you with this: evil-doers are trapped in the misconception of free will and free choice. They do have a choice to make this world a better place, yet seem wired instead for evil. I'm curious about how their path through life, their experiences and the choices they made, has brought them to this point. How do they get up in the morning and face the mirror, knowing what they are doing is destructive and morally wrong. With all of my *'strange stuff,'* I am happy that when I look in the mirror I know that I will make choices for the people without a voice – because I can.

Pause for thought

When you hear the term human rights what do you think? It hasn't escaped me that I am writing my book at a time in the world where many feel that their human rights are being eroded. What I think escapes many people, is what exactly is meant by our human rights, and how many people all over the world have been denied these over the centuries. Let that sink in while you read what is defined in the first four articles of the United Nations' *Universal Declaration of Human Rights*. It consists of 30 articles in total.

Article 1 of the Universal Declaration of Human Rights states that "*All human beings are born free*".

Article 2 describes how everyone is "entitled to all the rights and freedoms set forth in this Declaration, without distinction of any kind, such as race, colour, sex, language, religion, political or other opinion, national or social origin, property, birth or other status."

Article 3 is short and precise: "Everyone has the right to life, liberty and security of person."

Article 4 states that "No one shall be held in slavery or servitude; slavery and the slave trade shall be prohibited in all their forms."

Please read each and ask yourself, what does that mean to me? How do I follow these each day? How do these fit with my values? How can I be a person who respects the human rights of others? How do I claim my own human rights?

Ok, that's a lot of questions, but it's important that you know what is in this Declaration, otherwise it becomes just another set of important, but forgotten documents that line your shelf – dusty and neglected.

If, when you read these, you feel deeply that everyone should have their basic human rights honoured, then how do we make these important articles reflect reality, and are not just more documents stuffed into a law book?

This starts with becoming aware and conscious of what is going on right under your nose, and becoming that troublesome guest in hotels, who asks about policies for the employees, for those who built the hotel and under what conditions, interviews the cleaners about the conditions, etc. Hotels need to be shamed for allowing guests to order prostitutes and buy sex delivered to their rooms, right under the noses of management. This is not like ordering a midnight pizza, this is a blatant violation of human rights.

There needs to be supply chain transparency, for every product sold in the grocery trade, the clothing boutique and the construction trade. In fact, every business needs to be aware of what could potentially be going on in their supply chains. Supply chains are just downline providers, they spread like spider webs. Make sure when you buy something, you are not caught in anyone's web of slavery.

Before we sit down in the nail salon to have our "*beauty fix*", we should ask how the workers are treated, if they are fairly paid, and what their living conditions are like. Many people doing jobs like this are caught in debt slavery, where they will never catch up on the debt, because other people have control of their lives. Imagine having to wait for your freedom while you pay off some unreasonable debt. This is enslavement. It may look like a job, but it is slavery. Debt slavery is a big part of the modern slavery concept. We have the power to stop the demand for this.

Consider the following

The ring on your finger might symbolise love, but is most likely produced under oppression. Imagine knowing that your ring has been procured from the brutal enslavement of children.

Jewellery supply chains are, by their nature, complex. 90 million carats of rough diamonds and 1,600 tons of gold are mined each year globally. This generates over $300 billion in revenue, and is the daily work of millions of people. The conditions in which these people work are, in many cases, terrible. Children are injured and die at work, indigenous peoples are forcibly relocated, and land and waterways are destroyed, negatively affecting entire villages. Wars happen because of the human greed for these precious items. We can all be a little more diligent before being delighted with the sparkly gift we want to buy for a loved one.

Do you love that moment when you can sit with a cup of tea and savour your favourite chocolate? Chocolate is universally loved as a sweet treat. The taste of chocolate is one that is loved and longed for by many. Yet, it is a product that cannot often promise the same taste of freedom for its workers. Once again, there is little transparency in the cocoa supply chain. It is up to us, the consumers, to ensure that the chocolate we consume is ethically sourced.

Swedwatch[xiii] conducted an investigation into *Chocolate's Dark Secret*. This study shows the link between rich countries' consumption patterns and farmers' working conditions on the plantations in poor countries. Child labour is common on cocoa plantations, and results in heatstroke, injuries or regular amputations after machete accidents, poisoning due to pesticides and snake bites, in addition to long working days without breaks. They conclude that a fundamental issue is the price that is paid to the farmers.

It's Friday evening. You are happy to be home after a gruelling week at the factory, but you are delighted as you have got a brand new TV, straight off the production line. A gift to all of the senior management team for a great end of the year result. This weekend, you will get a few jobs done, mow the lawn, and help your partner put up the new curtains. And on Saturday evening, you'll be experimenting with a new rice dish.

It all sounds rather delightful, doesn't it?

Read what author Kevin Bales [xiv] says, and then consider your potential contribution to slavery.

It's quite sobering, isn't it?

"Slavery is not a horror safely confined to the past; it continues to exist throughout the world, even in developed countries like France and the United States. Across the world, slaves work and sweat and build and suffer. Slaves in Pakistan may have made the shoes you are wearing and the carpet you stand on. Slaves in the Caribbean may have put sugar in your kitchen and toys in the hands of your children. In India they may have sewn the shirt on your back and polished the ring on your finger. They are paid nothing.

Slaves touch your life indirectly as well. They made the bricks for the factory that made the TV you watch. In Brazil slaves made the charcoal that tempered the steel that made the springs in your car and the blade on your lawn mower. Slaves grew the rice that fed the woman that wove the lovely cloth you've put up as curtains. Your investment portfolio and your mutual fund pension own stock in companies using slave labor in the developing world. Slaves keep your costs low and returns on your investments high."

When we do not protest against what we consider to be wrong, we give our silent acceptance. When we do not vote, we ignore our ability to choose. When we choose not to see, we keep ourselves blind. In short, we lie to ourselves.

Chapter 11

I would like you to pass on our voice. It's not a voice. It's a cry of pain. We have been here in Lebanon because they not only raped us, they also raped our land and dignity.[xv]

Free your voice

"Prostitution is a form of women's empowerment and poverty alleviation. It should, therefore, be legalised and regulated by the state like, for example, in Denmark or Germany." We were at dinner when I overheard this statement being made. It seemed to me that this recurring theme was being shown to me, so that it would lodge in my conscious mind. What was it about this statement, or the people speaking to it, that needed addressing? I'd been thinking about it in connection with choices, and now it seemed to be about prostitution as a privilege. It made me wonder if the person who made the comment had ever met a woman who sold sex and, if so, under what circumstances? My first impulse was an urge to leave the event. Did I want to share more precious hours of my time with people holding these opinions? I came up with a thousand reasons and excuses to hit the road. I stayed, and on my way to the host couple to thank them and say goodbye, it struck me that this was a chance to make my voice heard. This was as good a time as any to put shyness and insecurity in the corner, and represent those with no opportunities to speak up for themselves.

Straightening my back and taking a deep cleansing breath, I crisscrossed between drink trays and the party people and tapped the person, who happened to be a man, on his shoulder and said. "*Excuse me, but I couldn't help but overhear what you said about women selling sex. If you do not disapprove, I would like to add some facts to the discussion.*" Three long seconds elapsed, then three more. It felt like an eternity. He excused himself to find some other guests to engage with in small talk. At times like this, I wish I were an actress with a clear voice, trained to deliver my message with clarity and presence. In my assumed character, I would deliver truth after truth with a steady tone and crystal clear articulation.

There have been so many times when my voice has failed me. As a teenager, I longed for a role in the school's musical theatre group. I thought that if I wished harder and harder that the director would pick me. That somehow, he would feel the vibration of my longing. However, because he was a music teacher and not a mind reader, I was never given an exciting or even vaguely interesting role, let alone the main character. I was invisible in the crowd - in the choir – and, so it seemed, everywhere. My body ached with boredom waiting around for my moment.

My dream was to sing beautiful duets, perform in the spotlight and receive deafening applause. As I sat in the audience watching, I became Mary Magdalene in Jesus Christ Superstar or Elaine Page's character in Chess. In my imagination, my voice was strong, clear and impressively powerful. As the applause ebbed out and we walked out of the auditorium hall, I shrank into my shell again, and fell as silent as a mouse. Stuffing my hands out of sight, I felt once again safe. If my hands were not seen, they could not communicate how I was feeling.

Hands are so important. They give, receive, and can call attention. There have been times when I wished I had put my hand up, like the time I could have spoken up for my classmates who were being bullied. It was the right thing to do, and yet, I remained silent. Children can be so cruel, and often see bullying others as the norm. This flows from the classroom and out into society. The worst case I remember was a boy in primary school who played the violin as a virtuoso at a very young age. On his nose, sweat drops formed whenever he became nervous, which he often was. Some of the guys in the class used to call him "*sweat-nose*" and other not so flattering names. I really felt for him but didn't dare to protest against this cruel psychological bullying. I did not have the pondus, nor the position in our class, to be the one to assert that this was wrong. Quiet, shy and diligent/ambitious were my epithets, according to my teachers. I think I was selfish, non-empathic, and a real coward. When our class reunion comes around again, I will ask him for forgiveness of my silent acceptance. The only consolation is that he is today one of Sweden's, perhaps the world's, best violinists.

According to the science of Ayurveda, a weak voice is a result of not being able to speak your truth, neither to others nor even to yourself. This was definitely true during my teenage years when I suffered from many throat infections. Curiously through each of my pregnancies, I have felt myself becoming balanced and healed. My voice, truth and throat have felt stronger with the connection to the new life waiting to come to earth, to take their place and speak their truth. Pregnancy changes you, and any mother will tell you that it creates a protective power within you, that enables you to give your voice to things that you might otherwise not. It is when I think of my children, I know that it was right for me to climb off the pedestal that was created for me, and use my voice to support others who are unable to use their own. They remind me of my helpless babies, who cry to be held, loved and nourished. Is that too much to ask?

I am reminded of another birth, the birth of Buddha, who has brought such enlightenment to the world. The Enlightened One cannot have escaped your attention, nor can the teachings and many sayings we see in the Western world. Despite having returned to spirit many centuries ago, his teachings continue to influence the lives of many across the globe. You don't have to travel far to see the way that Buddhism has become popular. Siddhartha Guatama, known as Buddha, was born in southern Nepal, a country boasting beautiful treasures, such as the second largest water reserve, the "*world's roof*", and Mount Everest in the breath-taking Himalayas. This little country also offers a variety of culinary delights, like paneer (yak cheese) and Dahl bath (the traditional lentil dish served with every dinner).

Then there is Tenzing Norgay, said to have been born a Sherpa who, along with Sir Edmund Hilary, reached the summit of Mount Everest in May 1953. From a very lowly background, he went on to receive the George Medal and other accolades from the Queen. What an honour he must have brought his family and country. Like Tenzing, Pasang Lhamu Sherpa also scaled Mount Everest, and was the first Nepali woman to achieve this. As you can imagine, back in 1993, this was an almost impossible dream for a woman who was expected to stay at home and perform womanly duties. Like many women born into poverty, she was a woman with a dream, spirit and courage who wanted to break free of the expectations of the caste system.

In 1962 the ideals of the caste system became illegal. But how can the law affect or override centuries of tradition, culture and custom? The complicated caste system separates people by class, religion and occupation. It divides everyone except the most enlightened, courageous few who see everyone as equal, with an equal right to live a good life. But having principles in a country steeped in tradition can be tricky to manoeuvre around. Especially when an illegal system of tradition still breathes stereotypical hatred into its people. At the top of the caste system, you will find the Brahmins, which often originate from priests, and are found mostly among well-organised and high-class families. Then the Chhetri, who are noble families often found in the military, administrative and governmental occupations. Next Baise and, finally, Sudra, known as the *untouchables*. If you are Newari, your parents are probably farmers, goldsmiths or involved in trade or entrepreneurship. Then there are the service-castes, the former *"unclean"* or *"untouchables"*, like the Kurmi, Lohar (iron-smiths) or the Dhobi (washermen), often very poor and treated with no respect. Imagine what this does to society.

Everything about a caste system equates to and establishes your identity. Stepping outside of your caste can mean castigation and isolation. Imagine not being able to marry someone that you love because they do not belong to your caste? Imagine being expected to behave in a certain way because that's what your culture has dictated. This is not about living in a society with laws, morals, values and ethics, or even a greater sense of freedom around these. This is about having a system forced on you because of the circumstances of your birth. You have inherited limitations, obligations and expectations, where violating the rules means social isolation or worse.

Next, imagine you are born into a middle-class family in a small village in Nepal. You are your parents' firstborn, which in any family puts a special light on every step you take. To honour your family and to be able to reach your dreams, you know that your education is vital, and you need to achieve the highest grades possible. Your parents have imbued you with their hopes. As they poured their love into you, they also dripped in this idea that your life could be different, and the chains that held them could now be released with your generation. You will be and become what they couldn't. They whisper to each other into the night that you, their firstborn, will bring change and good fortune to the family. You don't hear their whispers, but you feel the heavy burden of responsibility of their hopes weighing heavily on your shoulders. You know that you have a big job to do.

You hear your parents talking in their snatched time together. How can they ensure that you can maximise every precious moment of your learning? Although they need you around the home, they also know that they have to create opportunities for you to maximise every learning opportunity for you to be that change. They discuss the hours it takes for you to walk to school. Three golden hours of learning lost in just one direction. Six hours a day, five days a week, means 36 hours leached into the earth. But instead of planting seeds, there won't be any fruit at the end of this labour. Because they want the best for you, they reach out to the broader family and arrange for you to stay with a closer relative. Your aunt readily agrees to host you at her home. She too had dreams, and now she can live them through you, support the family and taste her lost education through your eyes.

Near your aunt's home is a hostel where you can study mathematics with the owner's son. Everything seems to have fallen into place. The son is ordinary. He has had the gift of education and understands how this places him in a position of power. Not that it's a power he wields heavily. He has learned the subtle art of abuse and getting what he wants, in a way that ensures he looks innocent.

And so it starts. The first time the son touches you, it is with a light stroke on your hair. You almost miss it. Then he starts to give you more and harder assignments than the rest of his students. You have to spend more time with him. This seems ok, and you become more familiar with each other. The second time he touches you, he seeks eye contact. You are not alarmed because it still feels so innocent. When the third time arrives, everything changes and his hands try to touch you everywhere, and his hungry look makes your blood freeze. Power. You try to escape the room, fight him, and then you surrender. He pushes you against a wall. You can taste the sweat from his palm on your lips. You let it happen. Afterwards, there is only silence and emptiness.

You have no one to tell because of the guilt you feel. You have no one to ask because of shame. Your only option is to return to your village, pretending nothing has happened and swallow your pain. Pain reaches far and wide around your body. It's in your stomach, in your head and your whole physical system. You understand that something strange and totally new is happening within you. Still, since nobody has ever spoken with you about how babies come to this world, you just go on with your life. Over time you notice that your body is getting heavier and weaker. At the same time, you feel stronger and invincible. There is new life pulsating through you. A new generation is being created, and you, like your parents, pour your love and hope into the growing child.

After nine months, you give birth to a baby girl, mirror yourself in her eyes and name her Atithi. But this is where the dreams die, and your family no longer holds you in high esteem. The sheen they once placed on you is tarnished, and you are forced by your family to leave your village, blamed for being unclean and untouchable. In their eyes, you have brought shame to your tribe by behaving promiscuously. They still love you, but their hearts are heavy with tradition, and they have no choice. You have to leave and make your own way in the world.

With your newborn, you make your way to the only place that can give you shelter – the temple. In the house of God and under his watchful eyes, your first dinner as a mother was some old bread salted with tears. Having no place to go, you retreat into your heart and tell your precious child that you will make sure that her life will be different despite the hopelessness you feel. Your soul rises to the challenge laid before you. You may not be a mathematics genius, but you are a channel for change. Right now, with a baby in your arms, it feels hopeless, but the flame of courage rages strong. Can you imagine what your life would be like if this were your story?

I first met Atithi, the child in the story, in 2013. The story is the story of her mother. Atithi now lives a long way from home. She moved to Warsaw to study with the help of ABC Nepal (a non-profit human rights organization). Everything Atithi does now is about creating the opportunities her mother was denied. When I talked to her about her life, she told me how she enjoys her freedom and especially hot chocolate with her friends. She knows that she is, by the power of grace, one of the lucky ones. She also knows that she was born into love but conceived through violence, a child of rape. The chances and choices that her mother didn't get, Atithi now has. She doesn't have to live in a village where she is considered unclean or untouchable. She enjoys what you and I do. She knows that she has these chances because of the love of her mother, who decided to fight for something bigger and better for her child. Atithi's mother used her voice to give her child a voice and a sense of place in this world.

When I recall Atithi's story and stories of many other girls I have met – the lucky ones – the ones to get an education, I know that I have to use my voice to help other girls escape from the clutches of those who believe that it is their right to silence them into submissive acts of violence, not only against their bodies, but also against their souls.

Pause for thought

We need to raise our voice, because...

... "At any given time in 2016[xvi], an estimated 40.3 million people are in modern slavery, including 24.9 million in forced labour and 15.4 million in forced marriage.

It means there are 5.4 victims of modern slavery for every 1,000 people in the world.

One in four victims of modern slavery are children.

Out of the 24.9 million people trapped in forced labour, 16 million people are exploited in the private sector such as domestic work, construction or agriculture; 4.8 million persons in forced sexual exploitation, and 4 million persons in forced labour imposed by state authorities.

Women and girls are disproportionately affected by forced labour, accounting for 99% of victims in the commercial sex industry, and 58% in other sectors."

This is why we need to break the silence, be uncomfortable at dinner parties, or wherever the subject of modern slavery comes up. Because right now, girls are being traded and raped, sold as child brides or cheap labour.

Because of the need to break the silence, we decided to support *ABC Nepal* (a nonprofit human rights organisation). Many girls here have personally experienced or witnessed this trade in humans, and now live with the trauma. The first visit to our sister organisation, *ABC Nepal*, was to ensure that our money was going to the right place. Some years earlier, our family had started sponsoring a few girls.

When we arrived at *ABC Nepal*, we were surprised that we were welcomed with wreaths and a dance performance. This tradition felt uncomfortable at first, because we did not want to be courted as higher-ranking people, but simply as friends from another corner of the world. But of course, these are people who are used to a caste system, despite this having been abolished.

The differences between the girls in Nepal, and us, are many, including linguistic, ethnic, cultural and socio-economic. This is easy to understand. Just as it was easy to understand that these were girls in need of schooling, a sense of belonging and an opportunity for freedom of choice. We did not see the reality of their everyday life, where they lived, and the environment that was shaping their lives.

We discovered how resourceful they are. They know how to get to meetings on time, despite traffic jams and non-functioning public transport. They know how to keep school uniforms clean, even if the gutters are full of debris and mud. They know how to navigate the educational systems and career opportunities, without challenging the traditions of the caste system too much.

Even though the caste system has been abolished, it does still live on in traditions and customs. Which, as you can imagine, continues to overshadow their freedoms. When I look at these girls, it makes me think about who really has a totally free choice. And how limiting choices can lead to limiting beliefs.

Back in the Western world, there are also families, social systems, grades, demands, and expectations that limit our choices. Of course, it's different, but I imagine that all of our inner voices chatter with the same judgments. The voice that says you are not good enough or doing enough. Maybe you don't hear this voice. Perhaps there are other words you hear?

What matters is that all of us do the inner work necessary to find our voices, speak our truth and speak for those who are unable to do this for themselves.

Chapter 12

When you own your breath, nobody can steal your peace - Author unknown

In the void

There are moments when life teaches you hard lessons. This is what most people want to read about, stories of adversity and miracles. Of how an underdog rises from the mud, and despite all hardship and circumstances, turns their mission from an almost impossible one into one full of possibilities and opportunities. As bystanders, we watch others make lemonade out of lemons and find that all-elusive happiness. I love a good rags to riches story, just as I can enjoy the happy endings so often delivered on the screen. It warms my heart and lets me forget what is going on in the world. The more years I live, the less I tend to enjoy these final scenes, when everyone is held and beloved and perfectly happy, and wonder - and then what? Then I am back from this idealised version of the world and happy ever after, and return to my mission.

Although I am happy, I still long for happiness. I think many of us are mental prisoners and trapped in our belief systems. We tend to reject arguments that do not support our beliefs. Therefore, as hard as it might seem, we have to challenge our thought patterns and find new drawers in our minds, like turning and facing the stranger in the mirror and getting to know that person. It's often the very first step that is the hardest. When I look, I want to know more about who the person is when they are stripped of all the layers *"keeping them safe"*. As we grow, we tend to pile up layers onto our core, as a shelter from the storms of life. It prevents us from being too vulnerable. However, it also inhibits us from being courageous enough to trust our own inner voice. Sometimes we touch this space without closing the lid, and right there, we are unconditionally happy.

It is right there, in the space of being, between doing and being, that somehow we find what we need to help us take the next step, and to have another chance at getting to know who we are. If you look in the mirror and imagine an emptiness, the stories seem to disappear. It's like dancing and the music stops, and the only thing left is the air around you. However, this emptiness is not complete nothingness; it doesn't mean that nothing exists at all. Some people think the void is a dark empty place full of nothing, a place where you are completely lost and, in a way, it is. It means you have entered a void where nothing and everything exists. There, in the void, you might find yourself and your life purpose. What if in the spaces are opportunities? The void is a place of infinite possibilities. It's a fantastic place and if we can learn to observe without judging, imagine what we can achieve?

You don't have to look into a mirror. You might find your metaphysical space on the golf course, while jogging in the woods, by the sea or racing your motorbike along a race track. It sometimes happens during a talk, when I am deeply connected with someone. Some of my more sacred moments in the void come when I encounter "*the big blue*" while diving or symbiotically making love with someone. Or magical moments while giving birth to a child. It is when I am there in the gap that I feel I am in another dimension. It's like when your body is left with no other choice than to go with the flow and surrender.

I can also see the beautiful woman who has spent the last fifty-two years building me a stage in the void. She keeps things in order and knows where everything is. When I get transported back in time to an event, it is she who can locate it in the albums. She sorts everything out, all of the legal stuff, every year, on time. She has done all the hard work so that I can be the ballerina, dancing upon the stage of life. She is personified by selflessness. My mother. The queen of kindness. She gave me permission to explore without borders and become an intuitive adventurer. My mother showed me that in the void, I could sit quietly and explore the furthest reaches of my imagination. I have memories from childhood where I am sitting on my bed daydreaming instead of getting dressed and ready for school. My mother let me be for a moment, understanding that I needed to be swept away by my vivid imagination for a while before entering the schoolyard with all of its expectations on how you should be. She intuitively understood that I found reality limiting and, at the same time, demanding. In my mind's eye, I saw a quiet place to sit and be. One day, much later, I discovered where this was.

It wasn't me who found Yoga. It was Yoga that caught me in its captivating manner. One morning in Thailand, when I dropped Olivia and Denise off at school, one of the other moms asked if I wanted to join her in her Yoga class. What I didn't know then was that she had pushed me towards a journey of love. I was not particularly impressed with the Yoga room, which consisted of a concrete floor with a broken metal roof. Through the cracks, the rays of the sun fell on the floor. Outside, the chickens sprang around the rooster, crowing as it suited him. On the only wall hung a woven image, depicting Yoga master Pattabhi Jois. What I didn't know then was that he would have a significant influence on my Yoga journey. It took a while before I got "*the Yoga bug*" and started practising Yoga every morning, eating vegan food and exploring Ayurveda, but what I immediately found was an inner peace without expectations or demands.

It was on the mat that I discovered what it meant to have an open mind. Unless you are open to ideas and perspectives, how can solutions come to you? It can be difficult to be pushed out of your comfort zone and consider the views of others. However, challenging your beliefs and thinking about how new ideas can give you fresh insights about the world; it can also teach you new things about yourself. I was hungry to learn more. I even ended up creating an equation for being open-minded. I added all of these things together - Science, Education, Experience, Wellbeing, Personal Development, Will, Solidarity and Karma Yoga - and decided that this was my equation and that I would need to keep it in mind, as I faced various day to day challenges.

It was here that I found my state of bliss, where there is nothing else but me and the Yoga mat. Bliss was where my thoughts became more evident, and the chattering in my brain quietened. If you turn yourself upside down in a *Sirsasana* pose (Sanskrit for headstand), you will gain another perspective. As the blood rushes to your head, it quietens the mind and prepares you for meditation. From this state of mind, many crazy and beautiful ideas are born. I am sure many never make it to the real world. However, some become real projects and turning points in life. One of those ideas was a rock music tour against human trafficking for commercial sexual exploitation. While in a moment of deep reflection, I could see this crazy event being played out. The mind, being incredible, took my dream and helped me to make it a reality.

It started with the intention to arrange a tour to bring awareness about human trafficking to the Swedish West Coast. We were living in Florida and enjoying boat trips in The Keys, a beautiful archipelago. The idea that had come to me on the mat kept coming back to me, especially while losing myself in the healing currents of the ocean. One thing led to another, and on August 1, 2018, we boarded the catamaran, *Dragoon*, with a rock band, a film team and t-shirts with the logo "*Sex is not a crime. Trafficking is. Stop it Now.*" Because we were still living in Florida when the idea came about, all of the planning had to be done from there. I remember walking on the beach in Fort Lauderdale, negotiating a rental for a catamaran, big enough to be well visible in the ports, when a friend announced his arrival in Florida. Thomas, a filmmaker, had planned a golfing week with his friends, and asked me if I wanted to meet and discuss film projects in Nepal?

Sometimes the plans of the Universe will coincide with your own desires, and things happen naturally and smoothly. Within a week, we had planned our visit to Kathmandu, a Catamaran Rock Tour 2018, against trafficking in Sweden, as well as a documentary film project. Looking back, I am astounded at the speed at which we executed our plan. But when it is meant to be, it is meant to be.

Six months later, we teamed up on the maritime island Marstrand, with the rock band, The Poodles, who delivered an unplugged performance exclusively for this tour. Our daughters, Olivia and Denise, accompanied by guitarist Kalle, were on board to warm up the audience. Can you imagine how proud I was that the family was not only taking part, but actually singing for the world to witness? Bosse, the cook, cared for our well-being from breakfast to dinner every day. Captain Helena and the film crew, videographer and producer Thomas, his daughter Vera, and son Loke, were in charge of photography and sound. Sofie became my wing woman, and booked hotels, restaurants and clubs to play at. It all ended with the rockers spending more time on the catamaran with us than in the hotels - but that is another story. In addition to reaching out with our message and playing a lot of good music, I am very proud of how well the team worked. During two weeks on board, we did not have any conflicts that we could not easily resolve. It is my hope that everyone left the catamaran with a happy feeling. These memories have a special place in my heart.

What made our Rock Tour 2018 against trafficking so memorable? It's funny, isn't it when you look back and ponder on what seems like the simplest of acts has, in fact, had all of the components of the open-mindedness equation (Science,

Education, Experience, Wellbeing, Personal Development, Will, Solidarity and Karma Yoga). The knowledge we shared is backed by scientific research, mixed with our own empirical studies and experiences. We created awareness and educated people about what we had taught ourselves during the last 20 years. Our experience, through travelling, finally turned into valuable information and knowledge we could pass on to others. Onboard, our team worked efficiently towards the same goal, most days in harmony. The film crew, with a solid background in filmmaking, understood what makes an enchanting, entertaining, engaging, appealing and informative documentary. Opportunities for our personal wellbeing were many, like morning Yoga, beautiful surroundings, plenty of good music, performed on stage or by jamming musicians in the catamaran's large cockpit. This, combined with Bosse, the cook's, delicious food, resulted in a feel-good-vibe. None of the above would be doable without the strongest driver there is, the *Will to Do Good*.

I will never forget the eureka moment that made this possible and the solidarity of all involved. It was over, and I was both exhilarated and exhausted. That meant it was back to the Yoga mat to see what might transpire for the new chapter of my life. I felt those familiar butterflies in my stomach, the ones you get just before you are ready to spread your wings, when your curiosity sets you free again. You know that this is the end as well as the beginning.

This tour put me on the stage, a place where I always longed to be yet, at the same time, I have this desire for solitude and going within, which I can do with my passion for Yoga and meditation. Eager to get back on the mat, I cannot wait to do some backbends to open my heart, and see if it is also a good day for drop-backs. Is this paradoxical? Could it be that the world is a stage? Just as Shakespeare says, all the world is a stage and we and all the men and women merely players. We make a brief entrance into the world, do our thing and leave as we enter. Or do we make brief entrances into our greatness, find our passion, perform and then one day be returned to some kind of normal life? In my wildest imagination, I feel that perhaps I am like a pregnant circus director, who wants to give birth to new ideas and perform them upon this stage of life, with my husband and children. Where, like a circus company, we can travel, discover new places and bring our ideas to life.

Birthing new ideas as we do, and making decisions to go to the places that need our energy, requires courage. When we set out on our voyages that arise from the void, we never really know what we will be a part of. It's like Forrest Gump's mum, who said it so well: "*Life is like a box of chocolates. You never know what you're gonna get.*" This is also true of everyday life, and for everyone. You never know where you will end up. Even when we are at our destination and working on projects, we know we will have to go back to Sweden. Sometimes sooner than I would choose. Like the times when my husband has had enough of the tropical heat and longs for the ice rinks. It's funny, because I know that my concept of "*mission accomplished*" never coincides with my family's. I comply, because these decisions are made in the best interests of our children.

One time, when we decided to come home early, we still had tenants in our home, and it seemed like a great idea to take a seven-week sailing tour in the eastern coastal archipelago surrounding Stockholm. This could have been a charming holiday, had it not been for the persistent rain clouds that had undertaken the task of delivering the whole year's water supply in just a few weeks. This was an altogether different kind of void. It was also the summer when I had been offered a role that led me to burnout. Instead of fighting for human rights, meeting inspiring people and creating miracles, I was on a highway to hell. Saying yes to this meant saying no to other opportunities yet, looking back, it was a *yes* to discovering the power of Yoga and being able to find innovation, creativity and spirituality in the void. I would never have learned how to pause my brain and fall into the golden well, from which magnificent ideas emerge. They say that the Western man's meditation is illness. Well, burnout is more than meditation; it is your soul telling you *no more you must stop*. I loved the healing I got through Yoga, which was when I felt energetically connected to my wholeness. Yoga training took me back to being and to my heart. And, since then, there have been many more ideas hatched. Yoga also invited me to record my ideas in my journal. I recorded them, knowing that one of them would undoubtedly come to fruition. When I flick through the pages, there is an entry dated June 2010 "*My life purpose is to use my femininity and strength be there for others and make a difference, wherever I find myself in the World*". You remember then, that in June 2011, twelve women graduated from our micro-financed vocational training programme.

Incredibly even today, I am sometimes afraid of what I might find in this empty space. To enter the void allows you to travel into your favourite image, be your favourite character, and experience the impossible, which can be transformed into something possible in real life. If it hadn't been for the void, I wouldn't have had the privilege of knowing so many inspiring people, working to end the demand that fuels the trade in human beings.

Chapter 13

"The fight for gender equality is the unfinished business of our time." UN Secretary General António Guterres

Passion

A soft wall of hot and humid air hit us as we set foot on solid ground. The contrast from the dry air conditioning in the seaplane made the sweat start to flow along our backs. A cloud of dust formed when the plane's engines spun up as if they could not wait to get air under their wings. The pilot made a 180 degree manoeuvre in the air, and returned to the mainland. Thirty minutes later, we found ourselves on a sandbank in the Pacific Ocean, a few miles from Papua New Guinea, looking out at the hazy horizon. Was this the place where time stands still? It felt liberating being in this gentle energy.

Our temporary home was a shack without walls, except for some load-bearing structures for dividing the bedrooms from the common areas and the outdoor shower. The tropical vegetation formed a beautiful backdrop to nature´s theatre. I allow myself to travel back. I am part of the scene every morning, as I slowly walk to my secret meditation place at the far end of the pier. It's here that I have chosen to spend the early morning hours. The only sounds are an occasional splash from fish that hit their tail fins on the surface before turning back out to deeper water. Everyone seems to enjoy it here. The turtle that crawls out of the sea to lay its eggs. The small sharks who tirelessly steal our fish just as we get them on the hook. They swim along with our catch, swallow it with the hook, bait and fishline. Despite the sharks' merciless hunting, there will be plenty of seafood left for us. Everything tastes delicious, especially the lobster cooked just minutes after it was collected under the rocks on the seabed.

When they defined the so-called blue zones where people live long and healthy lives, they must have forgotten to mention this place. If I settled here for the rest of my life, I would live to be at least 120 years old. Here is everything that makes my body work optimally: simple routines, beautiful surroundings, the magnificent beauty of nature without distractions and naturally organic food. The scrambled eggs from free-range chickens, who are allowed to pick the ground as they please. My breathing system is given time and space to complete each exhale, so that the inhalation follows effortlessly, as one breath follows the other, and it creates harmony in me. This is Haggerston Island. Paradise on earth.

When you come to a place like this, it is almost as if you are given a reset button, allowing your imagination to erase the bad memories and make space for something new. In the void, I find ideas and inspiration and, in this space, passion is rekindled. I am reminded of what is important. What is important is being and becoming rather than doing and doing.

While you are busy doing, you are missing out on the present moment.

I understand that I have to find time to stop and breathe, to be reminded of my mission on Earth. This is where I find harmonious passion. It is here, where all my core values have a party and go crazy. Curiosity is the key to having fun on a deserted island, where you can play Robinson Crusoe all day long. Expeditions to catch lobsters with harpoons, and sharks and dolphins playing around the boat, gives you adventure adrenaline.

This harmonious passion correlates with the mental state of being completely present and fully immersed in a task. Like nothing else exists. Research shows that this state is conducive to creativity. Psychologist Mihaly Csikszentmihalyi's famous investigations of *"optimal experience"* have revealed that what makes an experience genuinely satisfying is a state of consciousness called flow. During this flow, people typically experience deep enjoyment, creativity, and total involvement with life. The positive emotions and intrinsic joy that is associated with harmonious passion are what propel one to greatness.

At the other end of the scale is a passion that is not harmonious, and that is obsessive passion. Have you ever started presenting yourself as *"What You Do"* rather than *"Who You Are"*, defining yourself by criteria that represent your work? This phenomenon has to do with one's self-image. While harmonious passion is correlated with flow, obsessive passion is associated with negative emotions, compulsions, and an unstable ego. Passion that becomes compulsive is correlated with a negative self-image, including automatic subconscious associations between the self and the concept "*unpleasant.*"

Recent research found that online gamers, who were very harmoniously passionate about gaming, felt positive emotions while playing. By contrast, gamers with obsessive passion felt more negative emotions, both when playing and when prevented from playing. Do you feel a compulsion to work all the time, even when you really don't want to?

I do. Often.

My obsession has been dangerously close to crushing our marriage. I am aware it takes two to tango. Nevertheless, perhaps my wise father was right when he somewhat nastily said that he would not be surprised if I married more than twice. He knew me well, my father, maybe better than I knew myself. He was also brave enough to say it, reminding me to make my decisions carefully in the future. Perhaps he foresaw how my stubborn energy had the power to profoundly shake my relationships. I am interminably restless, and my ideal life would be to move every three years. I see life as a necklace of events, where each pearl has its own story of joy and sorrow, experience and adventure. Its value lies within the power and energy it has taken to chisel each pearl.

An incident that aroused my obsession occurred one afternoon in July 2016, at the US embassy in Stockholm. For the third time, we had been denied our visa application. We still do not fully understand the reason for the rejection. Seriously, what harm could our family do to the United States of America? With what motive would we start living as parasites on American society? We were an easy target for a zealous embassy officer, because our only reason for moving temporarily to the United States, was our daughter's desire to go to high school. Of course, I had my passion for change, but this time I wanted to give my daughter an opportunity first. We made life easy for the bureaucrats at the embassy, who were given multiple chances to use their power and put the stamp "*rejected*" on our applications.

Let me share the story from the beginning. In the summer of 2015, our daughter expressed her desire to attend high school in the United States. How could we possibly say no? During her childhood, we had pulled her and her siblings up by the roots several times, as we moved to foreign places without asking them. Now it was her turn to choose the direction. Since our elder daughter was already applying for musical theatre education in New York, we chose the East Coast.

Our dear friend and neighbour also wanted to come along on our adventure. We spent many dinners together planning how we would live our temporary life in Florida. Glamorous and sustainable was our plan. The final choice of location fell to Fort Lauderdale. At a rapid pace, air tickets were ordered, house hunting was scheduled, and application forms were filled out and submitted to all possible schools for all the children. We travelled to Florida and began to make contacts with brokers and schools, bought a house on Ponce de Leon Drive over the phone from Sweden, and fantasised about interior design and garden furniture. In our dreams, we wondered if maybe we should build a small dock and buy a boat to travel the beautiful canals of Rio Vista in Fort Lauderdale.

Only a small piece of the puzzle was missing. The Visa. It takes about two business days for someone to fill out all forms and upload them in the right place on the embassy's website. When this is done, one can book a time for an interview at the embassy at Djurgården in Stockholm. This was all done with relative ease. One month later, we stood in the queue at the US Embassy entrance with students, ice hockey players, and grandparents who wanted to reunite with their families in the United States.

It's odd how you can feel as if you are under surveillance by the security guards, even though you are entirely innocent. I must have known that all was not going to go to plan. We'd spent a whole summer collecting evidence that we were decent citizens who just wanted to spend two years in the US at our own expense. After what felt like an eternity, our number was called. The officer who would determine our fate stood at the counter. He held his head a little bit back so that his chin lifted slightly, making him appear to be looking down on us. Then the show was over before it had even started. In one sentence, he explained that our application was denied; however, we could apply as a business. We left the embassy beaten and broken.

In my usual way, I was determined that, after all we had been through, we would go and live where we wanted. My passion now became obsessive. For the next year and a half, I plotted and planned. I purchased a salon over the internet again. Employed a Swedish manager and prepared for her and her family's arrival in Florida. Not only that, my time was spent calculating salaries and budgets, looking for and hiring a migration lawyer, filing new migration applications, crying through many lonely nights with worries, longing for an adventure and watching my family falling into a limbo situation. It seemed no matter what we did, we were doomed to fail. I dragged my family through all of this, causing so much negativity, to the point that Stefan wanted to give up. "*If the US does not want us, I do not want them. Period.*"

I could not give up, and my fire was not ready to be dowsed. With my American friend and lawyer Lisa by my side, I was ready again with another potential scenario. This time our desire was to settle our estate, in other words, sell the house and salon. No, they said, that was not possible either. By now, two years had passed. Then Jan, an experienced lawyer with many friends in the diplomatic world, came into our lives. Long story short, she told us to travel to El Salvador two days before Christmas Eve, telling us that we would return 48 hours later with a 10-year visa to the United States of America in our hands. I still laugh at the memory of the rehearsal we did in our hotel room. "*You should wear a red dress tomorrow at the Embassy. That signals power*", Jan said. I didn't have a red dress, so Jan routed around my suitcase, making me try on and walk around the room as if I were being assessed for a catwalk show. She assured me, when I said that I felt under scrutiny and judged, that I was. However, this time we were able to walk on American soil legally and start our new life.

It is only on reflection, that I can now see how this kind of passion is completely at odds with the harmonious passion I felt while on Haggerstone. Yet, I could not stop myself. I can see that when I am living in harmony, our family thrives because I am at ease. However, when I am obsessive, I am at risk of losing something very precious. When in the grip of obsessive passion, you might feel that you are being focused and committed. The reality is that it's difficult to disengage, which can lead to burnout. Thank goodness I am blessed with my love of adventure and curiosity, as this gives me a second chance at harmonious passion, by doing something I adore. I look at this as doing things passionately.

Have you ever been paragliding? It is exhilarating. Imagine running along rough terrain, ignoring stones and other obstacles, fully focused on the moment when the wind and you are one. It seems impossible to be flying, yet here you are, rising like a Phoenix towards the blue, cloudless sky. What makes a man want to travel under the water or fly like a bird? Curiosity? Pushing boundaries? Adventure? Is it to feel the fragility of life to understand its miracles? For me, it's about mastering the hardest things to appreciate the simple events. The first time I managed to let a water ski split the surface at sunset, and dared to trust my balance, strength and coordination, I felt pure happiness and excitement. A few hours later, I walked barefoot up the dewy grassy hill with the water ski under my arm, grateful to have two functioning legs. Losing myself in this way, doing things that I love with undeniable passion indeed, once the thrill has passed, creates harmony in every part of my being.

I don't need to tell you that I am a passionate person who loves the feeling that passion can bring. One of my favourite feelings is the emotion that comes just before the departure to a new destination. Every new journey awakens more curiosity and the awakening of new knowledge. I always wonder what I will discover from the simplest things, such as which is the nearest school or Yoga studio, to more complex and exciting things like how does the political game in the country work? And then there are all of the other questions in between: how do we get in touch with the best surf teacher or extend our visas without doing "*visa runs*" every three months?

Being passionate can be fun, exciting and wonderful. Being passionate by nature means you tune in to a frequency that never rests. From the moment you open your eyes in the morning, till the last second of the day, before you go to sleep, that power is turned on. This is why I have now learned that I must take time out, either travelling or simply on the Yoga mat. I have to get reconnected. I have to get back to my being. When I don't make this space, I am in danger of getting caught up in obsessive passion, where I want more, I want it all, and I want it now. I thought this craving would diminish as I got older.

On the contrary, I find I am longing for more and more exotic travel, and harder physical challenges, but not in that crazy way of the past. Is there a diagnosis for this? I am sure there is. Until I am diagnosed, I shall continue to bring passion to my life and business for the good of all, and be mindful of when I am about to step over the line.

During a walk through beautiful Djurgården in Stockholm, this poem came up in my head. I think it mirrors humans' problematic relationship with passion.

It begins as a small, trembling flame. Deep inside of you.
You feel its lust, its desire to lead you.
You think you are capable, strong, beautiful and amazing.

As I write this, I am wondering how others experience passion. Is it through sex, perhaps love or emotions like joy or anger? Is it a potent force? Something you cannot stop, something you must do? Is that what those who are involved in trafficking feel, or those enjoying a pornographic experience? Are they doing things passionately, or has obsession taken them over. I know I do not view them through a suitable lens, because I don't feel that what they do comes from the heart. Passion, for me, is the heart of you, where this harmony I talk about lives. To me, the ones on the other side of the fence are controlling, not passionate. I can't imagine them being in love and feeling that kind of passion. I wonder if they would want to also control their lovers as they control their stolen humans? Do they even know how to be in love and share harmonious passion?

I can be curious forever, and perhaps never know. Just as I would never know what else they are passionate about. They could be family people and be as passionate as I am about education and educating themselves and their family. When I think about education, I am filled with excitement. Will I take another university programme, a two-day course, or will I get a divine lesson from a moment in life. I love to learn. I think it has to do with curiosity and control, appetite for adventure and respect for knowledge. Knowledge is power. Power facilitates survival. I get those who remain college students for most of their lives. After all, it is so wonderful to be always swimming in a pool of knowledge! The older I get, I find myself becoming more passionate about how behavioural patterns are formed. I have no academic education in psychology, but have learned a lot about how people work emotionally through my various courses and Yoga teacher training. I am aware of my stress and eating disorder, and my awakening to the people who now cross my path.

Not only do I wonder about those who have chosen to walk the gangplank and swim in a sea of porn, I wonder about you. How can I inspire you to discover your own universe? What arouses your passion and lust for life? Your anger? Your joy? When was the last time you shook your tail feathers and shone your light for all to see? We all have the peacock spirit inside of us, waiting to show the world the gorgeous creatures we are. What connects a heart to its owner? How does a gentle love turn into a strong desire? Has your passion been birthed, like mine, as I have realised the power of love, as each new life came into my world? Do your children inspire passion and purpose in you? Is it because of them that you want to make the world a better place? Do you feel the frustration, like I do, over fathers who do not talk with their sons about the difference between violent porn on the Internet, and the love they might experience when they treat girls gently and respectfully, inviting them to explore their sexuality with them? While Gandhi didn't say those immortal words, we have to bring our passion and love to the world, and be the change we want to see.

With Passion, nothing is impossible. Never Give Up.

The aspects of dignity and finesse have followed me as a shadow since childhood, when my wish for beautiful (read: very thin) legs was my dream. Afraid of my own strength, I have often turned them down and buried them behind a fragile facade. In my dreams I am a fine-boned ballerina with an elegant aura. When I dare to admit that my epithets are adventurous, curious and passionate, I have to put strength over dreams of beauty, and climb that mountain. So, beware human traffickers. I am so passionately ready for you.

Chapter 14

"If tomorrow, women woke up and decided they really liked their bodies, just think how many industries would go out of business." - Gail D

Vision

It is often at the top of a mountain that I get the clearest vision. The walk up gives me a chance to think, and it's as if the clouds clear just so that I, and I alone, are at the top of the world, and there is nothing to stop me. My vision is clear, or at least it is for just one day, and the next day I feel fearful because it's too big or too powerful, and who am I to be changing the world?

Then I remember that I'm the one who started all of this, and I am certainly going to finish what I started. I think of my legacy, and that scares me too. Imagine me being remembered for changing perceptions and bringing my work into schools, so that children could be protected from predators. Imagine businesses wanting to be a part of educating the world, or helping me to build centres that change lives. Imagine me being a pioneer! That's when it hits me, a vision without a plan is useless, and I stop staring into space and think about the practicalities. Where do I start? Is it in schools, or is it with some equally passionate sponsors, who may lack the time to do what I am here to do? This is when I know that I have to stop dreaming, start visioning and make a plan. That starts here.

My overall vision for the world would be the end of human trafficking which, sadly, I don't think will happen within my lifetime. Where would the supply and demand for human bodies go instead? The big picture vision is to slow down the demand and educate the children who can make a difference. Let's face it if young YouTubers, Greta T and Malala can get themselves onto a global stage, why can't our children? They are the ones supported by the people who will change the world. Didn't the Dalai Lama say it was the Western woman who would save the world? If that is so then, it starts with us, and we have to educate the children.

There are days when hubris catches me, I feel like I have total control, and I am in charge of my big plan. I have the power to break the vicious cycle, and I see clearly how to turn it into a healing chain. I mean, how hard can it be to educate children not to hurt other people? I believe that we can be the first link in that chain, and all I ask is that you take a look at yourself in the mirror, and start making that change. Then spread the message.

Then there are days when my confidence sinks to a minimum, frustration grabs me. I feel like a small child throwing a tantrum. Not that anyone can see that, but I am stamping my feet within. Of course, I will not stay in that mood for long because I have a mission. My dearest wish is that if you have read this far, you will join me in throwing off the mantle of *I can't* and contribute with whatever you can of your valuable time.

We can do this, can't we? We can start by slowing down the vicious cycle, in which the demand (for prostitution and porn) feeds the predators (the pimps and the porn producers) who prey on the vulnerable (children and young adults, the extremely poor, the refugees, the orphans, etc.), and turn them into victims of trafficking, so that the supply can meet the demand which, in turn, will feed the predators, and so on. We can create a healing chain. I believe with all of my heart that this is possible.

The healing chain starts with education for all children and their parents, and then spreading that awareness out into the world, through events and projects by grassroots activists, companies and NGOs, new laws created by Government and world communities, such as the UN and the EU coming together. If everyone joined forces and created one holistic team, this would lead to diminishing the demand.

The private sector has woken up with CSR (Corporate Social Responsibility) programmes. Add to that the many entrepreneurs who understand the value of responsibility and transparency, and we are part way there. With these by our side, we can create more awareness and enable the organisations involved to get a return on social responsibility. Corporate Social Responsibility is not about marketing, it cultivates the increase in wealth.

My aim also has a shorter perspective, which makes the end of the rainbow seem closer. It is to *do* something and to do it *now*. I love the inspiring sports brand, *Nike's*, slogan, "*Just Do It.*" My life purpose is to do what I can for those who need me right now. In Sweden, it is about raising awareness about trafficking, porn and prostitution, and renting apartments to women who need sheltered accommodation. When I find myself in a developing country, it is about creating self-sustainment, economic empowerment and opportunities for education. In all cases, it is about alleviating poverty. Economic poverty leads to higher criminality and an insecure world. Mental poverty leads to inner stress and anxiety, resulting in an unsafe life and vulnerable people. This often leads to greed, a destructive need for control and abuse of power. Poverty is, in itself, the cause of so many injustices and suffering, and often induces prostitution and human trafficking for sexual purposes.

In my aim to make a change, I also strive to reduce poverty in my inner world. I feel I lack the wealth to be entirely happy with myself and with life as it is. It is my quest to reach a place of harmony and leave my obsessive passion behind. I think I owe this to my children.

One day, I want to show them how grateful I am for life, as it is right now. It is thanks to them that I understand the preciousness of life, and what a waste every lost moment can be. If I can inspire my children just a tiny bit, and make them see that they are my greatest inspiration, then my life goal is reached. I want to look my children in the eyes and assure them that I did my best to show them that everything is possible. Therefore, I will never stop trying to reduce the demand for children's bodies on the market for sexual exploitation. Because no demand means no trade. And if you do not protest against this cruelty, you give the market your silent acceptance.

To realise my vision, I have to expand our team to go beyond the immediate circle of the family. My introverted side shivers at this thought, but I know I must do it. I've stepped out and allowed myself to be challenged by strong, inspirational women and men who can realise the vision, by interpreting the mission in their own way. Delegating a task, and then daring to release it, is like releasing a butterfly. If it is allowed to fly under its own power, spreading its wings as it glides with ease, it becomes more beautiful to view. Throughout my many different attempts to spread awareness, my conclusion is that, whether it is about rebuilding the infrastructure after a natural disaster, or developing a strategy against the child sex industry, we are far more successful through collaboration. The energy that arises when we create together, is challenging, if not impossible, to produce alone. So, where my philosophising and meditating in the void ends, the mission begins to realise my vision.

Sometimes I wonder if there could have been a more sustainable way to support all the girls at the centre we have come to know and support over the last decade. How could we empower them without sending out a bitter taste of pity? I have to keep in mind that Rome was not built in one day, and my vision will take more than a day to come to fruition. But then there are days, and there are days. One incredible day was when I was standing on a plot of land in Nepal. Staring out across the scrubby grass, I could see a building that was going to change lives. In this building, we would create:

A home for survivors of human trafficking for sexual exploitation, and vulnerable children at risk of becoming victims in the traffickers' cruel trading net.

A Bed and Breakfast where tourists can rest and acclimatise before heading up the beautiful mountains of the

Himalayas. This will bring income to the transit home/safe home for the children, so that they do not have to live on donations.

An educational centre, where:
- The children will have the opportunity to go to school
- The trekkers/tourists will be given information about the human trafficking situation, and how children are sold over the border to India, and to the growing sex industry in Nepal
- Groups will be welcomed to hold team-building retreats in the building, such as personal development, management or meditation

I had it all figured out and knew that it was definitely time for the next step. It seems so easy and achievable when it's put on paper. This is what I see, and so it will be. The part which I find puzzling, is how do I turn what I envision into reality? Even if it turns out differently from the one I held in my vision, there is always a path. In Chapter 15, you will see that I was struck with the realisation that, out of the blue, there could be a better way. But right now, this is not the case. This often happens, doesn't it?

There are many ingredients needed to make the vision come alive. Things like education, research, science, raising awareness, creativity, collaboration with locals, communication and listening, funds, building value, working at the grassroots and, of course, rolling up your sleeves and working.

An essential piece of the puzzle is communication. Communication is the hardest thing I know. My throat tightens as I remember the lectures at school when the whole class's eyes examined me and penetrated my entire being. It felt as if they could see into my brain and know all of my thoughts and secrets. I, the shy one who never said anything unless asked, desired to be popular and brave like the others. If I was going to open my mouth, I told myself, it must be brilliant, accurate, charming and fun.

Now, several decades later, with a throat chakra that is mostly healed, I am daring to make my voice heard for our amazing children. It is like a vortex has opened, and I have to be a driving force in the movement for social responsibility and change. For me, it is time to speak up.

One part of my visionary plan is to hold meaningful conversations with boys and young men about the link between pornography and prostitution. Someone needs to listen openly to their stories and experiences. These conversations would cover how we are wired, and how women feel when their partners watch porn. I remember thinking that one of my boyfriends kept watching porn because I was not enough for him. I know now that wasn't true. I wonder if he took it further if, perhaps, he became addicted and wanted more than the lighter stuff of our youth. I used to feel jealous of the porn women because they had his attention. That's no longer how I feel and, now that my eyes have been wedged open, I feel honour bound to share with others what really goes on. These women are not to be envied because they are viewed as reusable commodities. Just as we might purchase bread to satisfy our hunger, they are bought to perform and fulfil another kind of desire.

I have another hunger, and that is to educate and be educated. During Yoga training, we learned about the chakras, which is our body's energetic system. In learning about these things, I now know how to bring balance to myself, and why I need to restore balance in the wider world. It's the throat chakra that most fascinates me. I have my vision, and yet I feel my words lumpy in my throat. They want to come out, but they are joined by a knot of old beliefs that needs some untangling. Strange thoughts come in like, "*What if no one likes my proposals?*" Quickly followed by, gulp, "*What if everybody, like ALL PEOPLE IN THE WHOLE WORLD, like my proposal?*" On the one hand, being sensitive to the energies in you and others is an asset, but to bring about change, you have to let go of the feeling that you are being judged for every step you take.

Every journey I have taken has opened me up yet further. Can you imagine the excitement of arriving somewhere and then suddenly being filled with doubt about the new customs and languages? The uncertainty makes me both vulnerable and humble, and sometimes cynical about the cruelty that I see, which arises from poverty and desperation. When I try to communicate what I have witnessed to others, I often get comments like "*Oh, dear, it is awful*" with a voice full of pity, which just makes me angry. Pity has never helped anyone. Even worse are comments like: "*You must understand that the world has always been like this, and it always will be.*" My answer to that is, "*Yes, if we listen to people like you, we won't be able to change anything*". Then, as you may recall, we have the classic comment, always from a man: "*Prostitution is the oldest occupation, so it must be ok.*" I do not see it that way. I think it is the oldest form of oppression.

Here I am with my values, passion, purpose, vision and mission, and they are all useless without action and cash. That means I have to put on the magical slippers of the extrovert and go networking. Ah, the dance of getting to know, like and trust others with my vision and for them to feel the same way. Often it scares me when I think about how much it costs me to implement what my heart desires. It's one thing, my father, leaving me assets, but quite another to lose what he built up, so that I could have this incredible life. He is with me, guiding me to seek opportunities that create value. He taught my brother and me well. Teaching me about the value of real estate investment has been one of my greatest lessons which have given me a solid foundation from which I can operate. Of course, at the time of his great vision, we were too young and immature to understand what a gift he gave to us. I meet with him in the void where I hope he feels my gratitude.

Whether we like it or not, to make things happen, we need money. This is currently the fuel of our economy. I can see the pros and cons of this, but today it is an implicit fact that money talks. The word *money* - what does it awaken in you? How does it make you feel? How does it affect your ability to implement your vision? Money can stand for security, freedom, opportunity, stress, trouble or joy, depending on what role it plays in your life. It arouses fear and uncertainty in me, because I am so afraid of losing what I have. It doesn't matter how much it says in my bank account. I feel a constant worry about becoming poor. Although I know that this is an inherited behaviour, from those in our family who grew up in very scarce economic conditions, I find it difficult to let go of my fear. I get scared when someone else in the family (my husband) spends money on entertainment or other "*unnecessary expenses*" such as travel and expensive cars. I feel out of control because I cannot control his spending. When this happens, I make bitter comments and forget our marriage vows. My husband chose me, not money, which he has consistently shown me. Yet, I grow fearful when money is consumed rather than invested. It seems frivolous of us, when there is a world that needs saving. Some might even call me stingy, but I am afraid of losing the foundation from which I can build my vision. I want my money and investments to grow and grow so that, not only can I feel safe, but I can create a safer world for those who have been, and are being, sexually exploited. Sometimes, when it becomes all too much, and I feel like the cowardly lion, I just want to run away to a desert island and give all of my money to someone who can make it happen.

When the fear subsides and the vision grows, I can see the beauty in all of the small projects I have supported, and can invest in, and how that changes lives. I know that these investments will create a more beautiful place for the world's children to play in. Above all, children should be children and devote themselves to education and playful games that prepare them to become healthy adults with sound values. I'm investing in the future of the world. With *Do Good Now*, the return on invested capital will immediately be monetary but, in the form of fewer people demanding children for sex trafficking, and thus fewer children without a childhood, will evolve to become worthy of its name. And if we can invite more companies, business angels, social impact investors and wealthy people along the way, we can build a community of cool investors who can make a real impact. There has, to my mind, never been a better time than right now.

This brings me right back to the energy of now. To succeed with a vision, one needs to regularly refuel oneself with good energy. Life is not all about fighting battles; it is also about love and family. When we visit faraway places, as you have seen, we invest in things that help us to feel good and therefore recharge our souls. That might be a massage under an olive tree, or a rock-climbing tour in the Himalayas, which frees the mind so that new projects can ease their way in. Perhaps something like wakeboarding on mirror-shiny water pulses the magic of the world through you. Maybe it is during a romantic walk along the beach with the sand massaging your feet, that you can feel the excitement and wonder of being in harmony with something much bigger than yourself.

I cannot do much if I do not partly enjoy it. When trying to weave my dreams and vision into the fabric of life, it starts with a single thread of intention. It must be interesting and uplifting, despite the gravity of what I must do. I also think that you cannot change the world alone. You cannot bring good to the world without having some fun. Co-creation is an awesome power. That's how we are going to implement this vision. Therefore, I want to invite you on a journey where we can feel good and do good. What do you enjoy? What makes your heart sing? Tell me, and we will make some plans.

Chapter 15

"All in all, you're just another brick in the wall." — *Pink Floyd*

Another Brick in the Wall for Nepal

When you see a wall, do you feel an urge to climb over it, or does it make you stop? Do you consider it an inclusion or an exclusion? People build walls around their properties for safety reasons, security against criminality and burglary, to protect or care for the people and the possessions inside. We have prison walls to protect society, for those who do not stick to the rules.

Symbolically, a relationship that is crumbling can result in an invisible wall being created between two people. Or perhaps you have entered into a relationship with baggage, which creates a wall around your heart. In all kinds of relationships, walls get built. These can be physical, emotional, sexual and spiritual. These are usually to protect yourself and others. It takes time to turn these walls into more positive boundaries, or more constructive walls. When it comes to children, it makes sense to set boundaries for them.

Most parents know that it's in their children's nature to test their limits. Sometimes it feels like my children were born knowing how to do this. I am sure that I did it with my parents too. Of course, I did. These kinds of boundaries are good. When I think of the people that will live in the centre of Nepal, I would like to think that we can create strong and safe walls (boundaries) with the bricks, and then teach them how to create and manage boundaries for their lives. It feels as if we are building a future together.

You may not have heard of the giant rock band, *Pink Floyd*. Or perhaps you have had them as an integral part of your life. Whether you know them or not, you will know that music has the power to move generations of people to act. In the 1970s, *Pink Floyd*'s singer Roger Waters wrote the song "*Another Brick in the Wall*", which recounts the psychological traumas that the singer had experienced in his youth, which caused him to withdraw from the world. The imaginary wall he is building, brick by brick, separates and, at the same time, protects him from being hurt by the rest of the world.

When the team of *Do Good Now* sat down to plan how best to raise funds to build much-needed transit homes and anti-trafficking centres in Nepal, we had three purposes in mind:

1. a safe home for children who are survivors of the sex industry
2. a B&B to welcome tourists to generate an income to our sister organisation, *ABC Nepal* (so that they do not have to live off donations)
3. a sustainable information and education centre to welcome team-building groups who want to learn

more about human trafficking and support the centre financially. (Fundraising through awareness).

The idea was inspired not only by the song *Another Brick in the Wall*, but also by the many other iconic walls erected around the world. Take the Great Wall of China, for example, which is 13,000 miles long and can be seen from space. The Berlin Wall divided West and East Germany for over 30 years. Some people also believe Hadrian's Wall in England was constructed to prevent immigration and smuggling. More recently, President Trump wanted to build a wall between the US and Mexico to stop illegal immigration. During the COVID-19 pandemic, and the fact of Mexico's lower mortality rate, the Mexicans find the wall a not-so-bad idea. Walls are everywhere.

All of these walls were constructed to create boundaries, and not always of the positive kind. At *Do Good Now*, we also want to create walls and boundaries. The walls that we want to erect will keep innocent children safe, and provide much-needed education, so that they can rebuild their lives. Our walls will create strong boundaries, protecting the innocent from being smuggled across borders to be used as pawns in a dreadful game of abuse.

If history teaches us anything, then it is that most walls have been used to instill fear and keep people out. Our walls will be built from love, will create a genuine connection, and will work to break down the walls of fear in our young people's heads and hearts. Young people will have the opportunity to discover what a life without fear, and one where they are respected, is like. Fearless young people are more likely to become fearless adults. Imagine a world without fear. Can you picture what a peaceful place this would be? It is wonderful to be around young, courageous people who dream big. Without fear, young people will have the opportunity to discover what a life without the walls of distress/stress can be like. Courageous young people are more likely to become confident adults.

What comes to mind as a great example of this was my cousin's son's thirtieth birthday party. It was impressive to witness the ease with which these thirty-somethings integrated with generations far ahead of themselves. Was it the heady mix of strawberry daiquiris that kicked off the evening or the dry martinis skillfully mixed by our young bartenders? What made them so comfortable to share a party with both their peers and us, older adults? I choose to believe the reason was a mix of education, experience and confidence. The majority of the party guests had devoted themselves to higher studies, at universities and conservatoriums. They also had extensive experience from various activities, such as ski-bumming in the Alps, or bartender courses in Thailand and New York. One had built a summer cottage with his parents. Someone else had grown up in an international environment, where political science and international relations were discussed at the breakfast table. They all had diametrically different backgrounds. Common to all of them was that they had the successful combination of education, experience and guidance from the adults they grew up with. They were indeed a group of unprejudiced young people who recognised each other's knowledge, opinions and behaviours. I do not think they even reflected on whether their hearts or minds were open or not. They just were. They listened, talked, sang, drank, agreed, disagreed and hung out all evening with a rare sense of humour and respect. There was no doubt that they had had their share of life experience, personal development and education, which is why they now were armed with strong beliefs and values. Above all, they socialised with a rare open-minded attitude. They had understood what it took me half a lifetime to understand - that you can not change anyone else, only your own approach. And if you are going to change anything for the world, or anyone else at all, you have to start with yourself. To these young people, this seemed completely obvious. I wanted to stay in this youth forever. I felt an ounce of envy for all the adventures, passion and excitement they had ahead of them.

The day after this event, Yoga helped me to restore my balance. I felt a surge of happiness. There is hope for humanity if we, as adults, acknowledge and take responsibility, and do not give up until every young person gets the opportunities they deserve, through education, where they can explore and be curious. Therefore, the walls we build should be safe places where adults can be responsible grown-ups and children are allowed to be curious and adventurous. Where they can, in turn, become curious and beautiful adults, like the young men and women I met at the birthday party. I think we owe this to our future generations.

Our walls should allow children to let go of their stories without guilt and shame, and find their way in life. Our walls should provide them with the confidence to know who they are, and that everything is possible. Inside the walls, we must create a loving environment that they have probably longed for all of their young lives.

You may be thinking, why should I get involved with these children when I have my own to take care of? Over the years, as a mother, social events promoter, entrepreneur and activist, I have thought about this many times. Often I have thought, what kind of mother am I, who occasionally either pulls our children up from their roots, or leaves them to head off to pursue my work in trying to change the world? Let me answer. First and foremost, it is my intention to make sure that my children have everything they need first. My altruism has a limit; it does not equate my biological children with the children of the world. I'm egocentric enough to value them and their well-being more than anyone else's. In a natural disaster, I would save them first. Period. I would not leave them if they needed me, or if they did not have such a responsible and available father. I also believe that we have well-rounded children who, hopefully, know they are loved and listened to. Because our children are who they are, I can work to protect others who do not have so many opportunities available to them in their lives.

I work against the demand for child exploitation and oppression for two reasons. On the one hand, I am furious at people who take the liberty of buying a child, and allowing others to rape them, film the whole crime, and sell it to a porn site, or transmit it live to a paying customer, who just ordered something to fulfil his lurid fantasies. On the other hand, I feel that this is healing my own guilt and shame. But the most important reason is that I want to show the next generation, including my own children, that everyone can contribute to change for the better, take human rights to a new level, and start being more responsible humans. If I can inspire anyone by doing what I believe in, it is worth it.

The walls we intend to build with the help of loving and skilful people in Nepal, help me tear down my own walls of fear. The walls are what I have broken down inside myself to be a more honest version of myself. At the same time, we are breaking down the walls of silence and ignorance in society, enabling me to realise my vision. To stop the demand, we need to make everyone aware of what is happening. Because once you know, you cannot go back and not know.

Long before my vision became a plan, I was actually trekking in the mountains. It was while walking down the mountain that my vision turned into a plan and a mission. Earlier that morning, my body had told me not to step under the ice-cold water on the freezing concrete floor. But I had to. My sweat had frozen and melted on my body many times during our trek, and I felt so dirty, I just had to take a shower no matter the circumstances. I had a vision of what it would be like to be clean. I blended the ice-cold water with the boiling water, from the kettle I was given, to take to the shower room. How wonderful the few seconds were when the warm shower released my body from the dirt. It was awful rinsing the rest of the soap with ice-cold water, and then delightful to put on the warm, dry socks.

This was my first visit to the Annapurna Base Camp. Avalanches had destroyed the lodging at the top, which is why the Machapuchare Camp just below the ABC Summit, at 4140 metres, was always crowded. We sat back to back with Koreans, Germans and Indians, sharing food from the same pots, feeling like cosmopolitan global citizens. There we were, a diverse group of people from different parts of the world, aiming for the same goal, to walk the final kilometre to the Base Camp and watch the sun rise behind the Himalayan summits. My son and I had trekked to the Annapurna Base Camp to make a documentary about education in a different part of the world, showing how trekking, combined with education, can diminish at least some of the demand for human trafficking for sexual exploitation in Nepal.

We chatted about our dreams and the land we had been trying to buy to build on in Nepal. On this trip, it was just that, a dream and a desire, but I knew that we would soon turn it into something more. Not long after the trek was over, a piece of land was presented to us. That was when the vision seemed to become a reality. I knew that every brick that we would lay would be a brick that would create a better life for one of the children we had had the honour to meet. Finally, we could see a plan being carved out, and believe that it would now become a reality. We did not know then what difficult bureaucratic obstacles we would face, or how foreign investments would have to amount to several hundred thousands of Euros to be approved by the Nepalese Government.

Somewhere between Christmas and February's Sports Holiday, it struck me. Frustration is a mild description of how our team felt. We wanted to build protective walls for vulnerable children in Nepal, far away from our familiar neighbourhoods in Northern Europe. In the middle of the Covid-19 pandemic, when we had to reduce our interactions with other people to a minimum, avoid travelling and only meet via Zoom or Google Meet, we tried to launch our biggest and most capital-intensive philanthropic project ever. I began to understand that this was not going to happen. With a heavy heart, I had to agree with our architect and our programme manager to postpone it all.

We had planned this for so long. For around two and a half years, we had engaged an architect, a programme manager, a project leader, written about it in our social media channels, sent people to Kathmandu, trying to make this a reality. I'm left wondering what the outcome of all this will be? For the time being, we will not build another home for children in Nepal. In a way, it has been a blessing because we have been forced to sit back, take stock and evaluate. In that evaluation, we have learned the following:

1.   Land prices in Kathmandu are skyrocketing;

Everybody has a "friend" who knows what you ask for, or has an associate who can help you with this and that. Everyone can offer services of all kinds;

Here we made a mistake we have so often heard about; introducing our idea as "*the white man's solution*" as being the best, without stopping to ask the locals or bringing them on board at an early stage;

We are not there. We are in Sweden, thousands of miles away from "*the centre of events*". It is exactly 6.104 kilometres bird's eye view from Stockholm to Kathmandu. Geographical distances tend to become mental distances if one is not seen to be regularly present;

The real estate market in Kathmandu plays the role of the stock market, pension fund, savings account and speculation for every Nepalese who has any money to spare. The bubble is growing, and rendering our project high risk;

The drive was ours, not from within the communities who were going to use the facilities and actually operate it all;

The real need. We neglected to ask the experts;

The FDI we were about to invest in would need staff, organisation, income enough for salaries, maintenance and administration, in addition to other overhead costs.

The bottom line is that we were about to "*solve*" one problem by creating several new ones.

And now what?

The answer came to me In the sauna a few days after having toured a property portfolio we wanted to acquire. It contained properties where serious crime and gang violence existed. The municipality, which was the selling party, had a requirement that the buyer involved must have a social pathos. Bingo! It's us! A new vision began to take form in my head, with sketches about how we could reformat the whole Swedish migration policy. On my computer, Excel sheets were created, with calculations on how we could start a microcredit programme, together with the Swedish government and the immigration authorities, for asylum seekers and paperless refugees from war-torn countries. A new box was about to be opened, without another being completed or closed. A classic mistake was about to be repeated.

My lucky star stopped me this time. We placed a bid on the real estate property, and soon realised that it far exceeded our budget. Saying "no" to one opportunity means saying "yes" to another. The following week, an email reached my inbox, asking if we wanted to be co-investors in a sustainable project in Nepal.

This time we could finance the construction of an entire village, where there has been a history and tradition of bonded labour – and human trafficking for sexual purposes. The villagers themselves, who now live in sheds, will receive vocational training to build houses. They will be able to buy a machine with which they can make bricks. With this knowledge, they will then be able to take a job as a bricklayer or construction builder, earn professional pride, which they can pass on to their children. The children will have access to education which, in turn, generates self-confidence and independence.

What is needed is cement, teachers and capital, of which we will be responsible for the latter. It is all based on the premise that the local government will release the land and give it to the villagers. Our counter-demand is that all children should be allowed to go to school, and that everyone takes responsibility for the success of the project.

My original idea, that one well-off family can support ten others living in poverty, no matter where in the world we live, is starting to take shape in its own way. Distributing wealth in a slightly more equitable way is not rocket science, just goodwill. This is further proof that things resolve themselves naturally, when our own will is in flow and synchronised with that of the universe. All that was needed was a time of letting go and surrendering. Meeting resistance, first to realise that I have to change something in myself before I can make a change in the lives of others, will deliver a holistic social impact.

Lessons learned

You know when it's time to review your plans and look at things from a new perspective. Ask yourself: is it possible that a different approach would work better? Although it may feel as if events have come to a standstill, this is temporary.

Play, dance barefoot or do a handstand and make use of the extra time you've been given to rethink your strategies.

You may need to step outside of the norm and the mainstream, and embrace your unique beliefs and attitudes. Life changes often come unexpectedly, and test your confidence and trust. Sometimes you need a co-driver who can compensate for your weaker traits and inclinations. You will meet with your teammates when you show your true colours and live by your values. Authenticity is unconquerable. When you speak, think and act from a place of honesty and integrity, others are irresistibly drawn to your sphere.

For the past two years or so, I have had sleepless wolf hours when anxiety takes a good grip on my heart. Accompanied by my heavy heartbeats, I have searched for a strategy to find co-investors in my expensive philanthropic projects. In the middle of an inhale, the universal will coincides with my vision - to invest with a return that benefits future generations. When we dare to let go and surrender to the kind people around us, small miracles happen. Now, I have had the honour to meet with someone else who has thought, evaluated and worked hard to identify the needs. Now they are looking for us. This means we are allowed to take a respite from stress, while we can feel good and do good. The circle closes, and our own motto comes to meet us with open arms.

This adventure has a new spectrum of real colours, in the form of solid knowledge, a team with experience, according to values that sound right when we talk about them. This is an external change brought about by an internal understanding. I believe it is possible to stop the demand for human trafficking if human responsibility is taken on several levels in society.

It is time to stop longing to be part of positive world development and start rolling up your sleeves. To be of any use, you need to dig where you stand. I use my entrepreneurship and financial resources as catalysts for change. Starting from your core values is both the easiest and the most difficult. You must show your true colours and be authentic. It's easier if you like *who* you are or dare to be *how* you are in all given situations which, for me, means to be adventurous, passionate and curious. It's getting better and better because I decided it's going well. Period.

Parents - we need you to talk to your children and, above all, listen to what they have to say. From the moment you meet their newborn gaze, they teach you loads of wisdom.

Schools - make human rights a major school subject, where self-management, empathy and human responsibility are implicit components. The next generation depends on your teaching values.

Companies - we need your transparent CSR (Corporate Social Responsibility) programmes to be implemented and understandable for every employee, so that they can proudly spread your values.

Governments - we need you to enact laws banning modern slavery in general, and human trafficking in particular, in practice and in theory. Society needs to show that enslavement in any form is never acceptable. Set boundaries that are easy to follow at an early stage, and prevent innocent children from becoming adult criminals in the cradle, literally. Make sure that not a single child needs to be part of a criminal network or become a perpetrator.

The Police - give them more resources so that they can keep up their good work of identifying traffickers and save survivors.

Journalists - keep using the writing power, exploiting the freedom of the press.

My contribution to the world stems from my inner journey. From there, I have a greater chance of working for an empathic world without human trafficking.

You've read my story this far, which means I no longer feel alone. For this, I feel a humble gratitude, free from guilt. Thank you.

Chapter 16

"It was never your fault no matter what, so let go of the toxic shame - it doesn't belong to you. You are never too old, too lost or too broken to begin healing today. Hope is the key, and even if it starts out small as a mustard seed, nurture hope - it will save you. And most importantly - you are not alone, you are not alone, you are not alone." Judge Robert Lung Survivor and Former Member of the U.S. Advisory Council on Human Trafficking

Breaking the Wall of Shame

As discussed in this book's first chapter, a sense of scarcity drives the economic demand for goods and services. Many of us, who are financially more privileged, try to dampen our sense of shame, boredom or emptiness by consuming and constantly demanding new, stimulating experiences. On the other hand, there are those who are forced to work long hours, with their hands and bodies, to create a supply to meet this demand.

Everyone who has been touched by human trafficking will have suffered the psychological effects of shame and combined that with guilt. As a result, they may feel that they are not worthy of help, or they may support and blame themselves for their suffering. Unfortunately, this means that for many, they will remain trapped behind their wall of shame.

When I started this book adventure, I wanted to inspire you by telling my story. I wanted to empower you to change whatever you wished to do differently in your life. And here I am, in the midst of everyday chaos, with never-ending requirements and specifications that must be met. Who am I to motivate you? I who, most of the time, am running around, trying to find my keys, shouting, "*Has anyone seen my Yoga mat?*", and who is always running late for the next meeting. I, who can never say "no", leading to zero hours for contemplation and evaluation. You see, I always try my very best, and that is what I want people to say about me when I am dead. And, yes, one more thing... That I tried to break down the walls of shame. Because...

At a young age, I experienced a judgmental opinion about my body from a person I held dear. He carelessly told me I was not as beautiful as my mother. He might not have meant to hurt me but, as a small girl trying to find answers to her questions about how to be and act in this world, this was an abusive assault. I felt such shame about being judged and seen just as a body. From my perspective, I was judged because I did not have as flat a stomach as my mother. From that moment until very recently, I have constantly pulled my stomach in, even when alone. For a great part of my life, I was convinced that one must be beautiful to be a woman who counts. Beauty was equal to having a ballerina's body.

Occasions like this result in hang-ups and low self-esteem. The most effective way to heal oneself and the world around us is through compassion and generosity, being, embodying and sharing the very best version of myself whenever possible. I don't know of anything that has the power to transform us, quite like the freedom gained through acts of kindness, whether it be a Yoga backbend, or an act leading to positive change.

Everything starts with us. I've said it often enough that you cannot change others, so it has to start with oneself. I understand with all of my being how important it is to try to treat others with a touch of softness. It is easy to project fears, beliefs, judgements, mistakes and negative thoughts about ourselves onto others. We have to step back and recall the vulnerability in our own hearts. This means confronting the shame when it knocks on our door, breathing through it and letting it dissolve. This also means ditching the guilt of not being enough and seeing that this is not the truth.

Where we get the strength to take human responsibility depends on our subpersonalities. How you want to show up in the world, and how your values motivate the responsibility you want to take, is up to you. You can only fundamentally change something after you have made that change in yourself. We believe in grounded thoughts and rooted ideas, which someone communicates with a confident voice. When that happens, the simplest two-dimensional drawing can be the seed to transform into a *do-good-now* project and change the world.

Luckily, we all have different perspectives and preferences, which change over time. Therefore, our responsibility is to decide how we want to appear in this world. Through tangible work against dependence and poverty, my aim is to do my best in all the roles of my life, and appear with love in this world.

As a mother, I want my children to be confident and say that they are happy to be who they are. Why? Because I love them and would die for each and every one of them. But also because they will soon be adults. Happy adults are kind adults. Kindness needs no reward, for it brings happiness and warmth to the heart.

As an adventurer, I want to travel to the deepest jungles, climb the greatest mountains, cross the widest oceans and jump off the tallest cliffs. I want to see so much more before I die. So I either need many more years or to start prioritising what I want to do.

As a leader, I hope to inspire with curiosity and an open mind, so that others can explore beyond their current environment.

As a writer, I wish to publish books to inspire and motivate others to join the movement against modern slavery. Yet it takes me forever to finish even one book, because a part of me is afraid no one will want to read it.

As an investor, my purpose is to add value. I have the ambition to devote resources to projects, which lead to real social impact. I hope to motivate other investors into taking social responsibility globally, from their environmental footprint to gender equality and working conditions.

As a wife, I want my husband to be proud. I hope he meets himself in the mirror, thinking that he made the right decision by choosing me as his life partner.

As a friend, I want to be present and listen, hold hands and share good and bad times.

As a global citizen, I hope we will stop talking about "us" and "them" without understanding that it is all us, our world and our time on earth. Imagine a world where people believe in CONversation, not ONEversation. Where people understand that UNITY and commUNITY are important for development. Imagine if we can inspire every child to understand how to be a productive and confident global citizen, and what that means, and motivate them to find their voice, speak their truth and feel confident to do so.

As a Yogi, I hope to gain the strength to fight injustice, to have the endurance to keep going, and the flexibility to adapt to different situations. Finally, I strive for acceptance, because change sometimes takes time.

As the completely ordinary person I am, I know my story is no better or more extraordinary than anybody else's. We are all of the same kind, and can do whatever we set our minds to, with a touch of our own unique colours and values.

Do what you love for those whom you love. Because nothing else matters.

For anyone who has not found their voice, I want to lend mine. For those who do not have a free choice right now, I hope you will join me in creating freedom. I will continue to strive to build value to combat the most shameful phenomenon of our time: Human Trafficking.

Celebration and next steps

So far, you have read about many of our excursions and adventures, and now would seem like an appropriate time to summarise what we have actually achieved. I couldn't fit all of these into every story. Instead, I'd like to show you just some of the things we have achieved. Paradoxically, I am both pleasantly surprised and disappointed when I read the list. Is this all we have achieved? On a more beautiful day, I can be amazed at how much we have accomplished. How did we manage to do all of this? The answer lies in that, as each task or challenge presented itself, we just did it. If we can all just do one thing and then another, we will all be able to make an impact. And, as with us, the impacts can take years. That doesn't matter. What matters is that we all join together to make a difference in some small way. What strikes me is how we take journeys in life, and rarely do we grasp or recognise just how far we have come. Celebrate what you have achieved, don't stop and don't be complacent.

The impact

These are the impacts made during and following our own personal family adventures:

2005-2007: 297 family providers and entrepreneurs in Koh Phi Phi and Koh Lanta in the Thai archipelago were able to rebuild their lives after the tsunami disaster, with Microloans from the *Swedish Microcredit Foundation*, administered by *Do Good Now* during 2006-2007.

The family members of the above-mentioned entrepreneurs benefited from this through all kinds of business opportunities. This gave them the chance to earn a salary again, provide for their children, and the possibility of regaining a belief in the future.

A one-year adventure, and a time out for our family, which contributed to our personal growth as global citizens.

International education for our children, which also broadened their horizons, and gave them a better understanding of other cultures.

A thorough understanding of the sex industry in Phuket, Thailand, meant that we were able to contribute more effectively.

These things changed our lives forever, and ignited our mission to fight trafficking for sexual purposes. We can never rewind and unknow what we have learned. This resulted in workshops in Swedish schools about modern slavery, other adventures and projects against human trafficking in Costa Rica and Nepal, and the content of this book.

Sweden:

Apartments provided for five refugee families and several women in need of sheltered housing. This has helped them to stay safe from perpetrators, gain confidence and build their new everyday lives.

Job opportunities for garden and painting work for eight people, as an alternative to begging outside our local shop.

30,000 SEK to *Hand in Hand* (www.handinhandsweden.se), a non-profit organisation working with entrepreneurs, as an effective, long term and sustainable way to reduce poverty.

Fundraising events to support the work against human trafficking.

A rock tour with the band *The Poodles* along the Swedish West Coast on a Catamaran, which raised awareness about human trafficking.

Uganda:

One orphan boy in Uganda was sponsored through *SOS Children's Villages*. He was offered a home in a village, with a mother and siblings, education, and nutritious food, which gave him a greater sense of belonging. This resulted in him later being able to live independently.

Costa Rica:

Through vocational training in beauty care, manicure, pedicure, facials and SPA massage, local women were empowered to become businesswomen and serve their communities. Not only that, they were able to offer beauty services to tourists. This education project was micro-financed and open for Nicaraguan and Costa Rican women in Guanacaste, Costa Rica. Instead of cash, we lent education, with which the women could earn a profession, and a sustainable way to make a living. The impact was many very happy women, liberated from working under slave-like conditions. The net result was a growth in pride, independence and a sense of self-worth.

One girl in Costa Rica was sponsored through *SOS Children's Villages*. She was offered a home in a village with a mother and siblings, education, nutritious food, and a greater sense of belonging. This resulted in a schoolgirl having promising future opportunities as an educated potential future entrepreneur.

Thailand:

One year's voluntary work supported 297 entrepreneurs and family providers recovering from the tsunami disaster in 2004. (Through the *Swedish Microcredit Foundation*).

Nepal:

Financial support of USD 25,000 per year, to *ABC Nepal*, enabling the girls who escaped forced prostitution, or were at risk of falling victim to human trafficking for sexual exploitation.

For *Build Up Nepal*, we provided financial support of USD 6,000 for new school toilets. This comprised the total building costs for toilets in a school. This is important for children, especially girls, who cannot gain a basic school education due to poverty and poor school support.

For *Build Up Nepal*, we provided financial support of USD 60,000 for the construction of a village. This is important because millions of families in rural Nepal live in deep poverty and are forced to migrate from their villages due to a lack of jobs, housing and economic development. These people are at high risk of becoming bonded labour, and being traded by human traffickers.

Build Up Nepal is on a mission to break the vicious poverty cycle in rural Nepal through safe housing and local jobs for poor families. Their mantra is building their way out of poverty. They specialise in CSEB Interlocking Bricks technology, helping the village members produce bricks and build low-cost, eco-friendly houses. A positive side-effect is vocational construction training with future job opportunities for the members of the village.

Which country *sparks* your curiosity and your interest to learn more? If you were about to volunteer, in what field would you choose to put your time and energy? What lights your inner fire? Which injustices do you want to crush first?

Author's profile

Ulrika Lorenz's motto is *Do Good, Feel Good*. As a philanthropist and founder of *Do Good Now,* she has devoted large parts of her life to projects that make a difference. She writes to raise awareness about human trafficking and other crimes against human rights. Through her work, she hopes to inspire others to find good social initiatives to support.

Ulrika's enthusiasm for connecting with the outside world and doing good, started early in her career, while she was at the Ministry for Foreign Affairs in Sweden in the early 1990s. Since then, she has become an entrepreneur, who has chosen to use a large proportion of her personal wealth to invest in a future with less poverty, especially in a world without slavery.

Projects that Ulrika has personally been involved in:

- Housing and integration of refugees and women from abusive relationships in Sweden, her home country, 2015 to present.
- Education project in Costa Rica, Micro-financed Vocational Training for Women, 2011.
- Financial support and work against human trafficking and sex slavery in Nepal, 2010 to present
- One year of voluntary work in Thailand to rebuild the infrastructure after the Tsunami disaster, 2006-2007 (in collaboration with the Swedish Microcredit Foundation).

Ulrika believes that everybody can be inspired to do good. What goes around comes around, and every single individual can do something to make this world a better place. She is determined to do anything she can to raise awareness and be a catalyst for other people to take action. This could be anything from teaching mindfulness and Yoga, to sharing knowledge, raising funds, housing a refugee, or helping to rebuild a house after a natural disaster. She thinks it is time to take human rights to a new level and start talking about human responsibilities. Ulrika is passionate about connecting with people and projects that are making a difference in the world, to help people to find a good cause, in which to get involved, and celebrating the good that is done, every day.

This is a platform where you can get involved with the sole purpose of Do Good Now.

Email: ulrika@dogoodnowglobal.com

Website: www.dogoodnowglobal.com

Instagram: @dogoodnowglobal

LinkedIn: https://www.linkedin.com/company/do-good-now/

Facebook: https://www.facebook.com/groups/dogoodnowglobal

Acknowledgements, Thank you and Namaste

This book would not have come about without you, Dale. When it looked dark in my writing heaven, your coaching and support gave me the energy back time and time again. The fact that you wrote many books, of which knowledge you wanted to share, I am humbly grateful.

To the Do Good Now Team, led by the structural artist Eva, keep up your great work and attitude. We are in this together!

To all of you who read early versions of the book and have contributed with highly appreciated feedback, I want to send a bunch of imaginary flowers.

Charlotta who went through the texts between the chapters and made sure they made sense as well as creating a lead page on our website.

Steffie who proofread when the rest of us were tired of all the words and made sure that the text flowed without changing my tone of voice. A big thank you!

Gunnel, you are a very intelligent and inspiring lady with life experience and dignity.

Zen, I love when you asked me the relevant question, "Do you want this book to be that biographical?". Thank you for that. You made me dig into the facts.

Deborah, my European friend in Florida, who stands by me in everything I do. Your feminine charm inspires me.

Louise, my crazy author colleague and friend, you make this world a happier place and motivates me to keep going.

Cousin Micael, you are always encouraging and full of new ideas. Thank you for the valuable notes in this book's margins, our long "walk and talks", and for giving me modern perspectives on things.

Denise, my personal trainer and friend, thank you for pushing me outside my comfort zones over and over again and for questioning my former book titles.

Hélène, whose heart rejoices with me at success and cries empathetically when I am sad. Thank you for creatively coming up with the title during one of our precious girls' weekends last summer.

Stefan, I do not know how to thank you for half a lifetime. I have deep respect for what you in action show what I mean to you. By the way, the book is ready now.

Thank you, Vincent, for coming with me to Nepal, climbing mountains and making a film. You are an actor and a gentleman, as well as the best big brother anyone could wish for. Leon, our fourth miracle, I think you agree. Thank you for enriching our family and spreading joy every day.

I feel the greatest admiration for Denise and Olivia, my dear daughters who teach me lessons every day, literally. Who else would tell me that I act like an egocentric, pathetic middle-aged woman or lift me up when I get too hysterical over life's minuscule obstacles. If I were your age, I would cut my right arm to be your friend.

Finally, Mom and Dad. You, Dad, are no longer with us in this dimension, but your heart goes on within us while your wise admonitions and street-smart comments rest in our memories. I hope you can feel my appreciation wherever you are. You, Mum, who I have the privilege to live close to, and who steady like a rock listens to my frustration over that life is not a dollhouse where all dreams come true. Thank you for your strength and for building the stage on which I get to dance.

References

[i] https://www.youtube.com/watch?v=_YpHNImNsx8

[ii] Source: United Nations Protocol to Prevent, Suppress and Punish Trafficking in Persons, especially Women and Children

[iii] https://marianne.com/a-return-to-love/

[iv] https://fightthenewdrug.org/get-the-facts/

[v] Source: Article by Nicholas Kristof, Opinion Columnist, The Ecomomist, Dec. 4, 2020

[vi] https://www.axios.com/pornhubs-video-purge-legal-riddle-7ce822bf-03b6-4d72-bb2d-fe482e0b6fc1.html

[vii] Gail Dines, Growing Up in a Pornified Culture | Gail Dines | TEDxNavesink

[viii] Malala Yousafzai, I Am Malala: The Story of the Girl Who Stood Up for Education and Was Shot by the Taliban

[ix] *Source: https://www.unodc.org/documents/human-trafficking/UNVTF_fs_HT_EN.pdf*

[x] https://www.icaew.com/technical/legal-and-regulatory/modern-slavery

[xi] https://tidningensvenskpolis.se/arkiv/hallarsida-aldre-artiklar/2016/nr-32016/simon-haggstrom-om-/

[xii] https://nordicmodelnow.org/2020/12/01/the-nordic-model-the-best-approach-to-tackling-prostitution/

[xiii] *Source: Swedwatch.* https://swedwatch.org/region/the-dark-side-of-chocolate/

[xiv] Kevin Bales http://www.kevinbales.net/

[xv] —Male survivor of conflict-related sexual violence in Syria, February 2019

[xv] *Source:* ILO International Labor Organisation, Global Estimates of Modern Slavery: Forced Labour and Forced Marriage, Geneva, September 2017.

Additional references

Chapter 4

https://porrfribarndom.se/porrsnacket/
https://fightthenewdrug.org/get-the-facts/
https://parents.culturereframed.org/

Chapter 8

https://itsusync.com/different-types-of-brain-waves-delta-theta-alpha-beta-gamma-ezp-9

Chapter 10

Source: Human Rights Watch
https://www.hrw.org/report/2018/02/08/hidden-cost-jewelry/human-rights-supply-chains-and-responsibility-jewelry

Other reading

Bales, Kevin, Zoe Trodd & Alex Kent Williamson (2009) Modern slavery beginners guide

An Inquiry into the Nature and Causes of the Wealth of Nations - 1977 Authors: Adam Smith, Cannan Edwin, Stigler George J.

https://www.ohchr.org/Documents/Publications/FS36_en.pdf
https://www.forbes.com/sites/ewelinaochab/2018/07/26/human-trafficking-is-a-pandemic-of-the-21st-century/#342076876195

https://www.theodysseyonline.com/crash-human-trafficking https://theanatomyoflove.com/

https://www.ohchr.org/Documents/Publications/FS36_en.pdf

https://www.yourbrainonporn.com/

https://fightthenewdrug.org/

https://www.nytimes.com/2020/12/04/opinion/sunday/pornhub-rape-trafficking.html

https://www.state.gov/wp-content/uploads/2020/06/2020-TIP-Report-Complete-062420-FINAL.pdf

Walk Free Foundation GSI rapport 2018 https://downloads.globalslaveryindex.org/ephemeral/GSI-2018_FNL_190828_CO_DIGITAL_P-1615802304.pdf

ILO, Walk Free Foundation (2017), Global Estimates of Modern Slavery, Geneva 2017

https://www.ilo.org/wcmsp5/groups/public/---ed_norm/---declaration/documents/publication/wcms_243391.pdf

UNODC Global Report on trafficking in persons 2020 - https://www.unodc.org/documents/data-and-analysis/tip/2021/GLOTiP_2020_15jan_web.pdf

Trafficking in persons report 2020 SWEDEN - https://www.state.gov/reports/2020-trafficking-in-persons-report/sweden/

https://www.etc.se/debatt/hellre-ruttnande-bar-modernt-slaveri

https://www.arenaide.se/wp-content/uploads/sites/2/2014/12/2014-Villkoren-for-sv-barplockare-%E2%80%93-Mats-Wingborg.pdf

https://www.byggnads.se/aktuellt/2014/ar-det-verkligen-sa-illa-som-det-sags-/

https://urplay.se/program/217956-ur-samtiden-ekonomi-och-mynt-modernt-slaveri-i-sverige-och-varlden

https://www.svt.se/nyheter/granskning/ug/uppdrag-granskning-avslojar-nagelskulptorer-blir-utan-stor-del-av-sin-lon-tvingas-betala-tillbaka-till-arbetsgivaren

https://www.svd.se/victoria-sald-som-sexslav-till-sverige

https://media.business-humanrights.org/media/documents/fb7a2e03e33bcec2611655db2276b4a6a086c36c.pdf

Made in the USA
Columbia, SC
26 November 2021